PUBLISHED BY BOOM BOOKS

boombooks.biz

ABOUT THIS SERIES

.... But after that, I realised that I knew very little about these parents of mine. They had been born about the start of the Twentieth Century, and they died in 1970 and 1980. For their last 50 years, I was old enough to speak with a bit of sense.

I could have talked to them a lot about their lives. I could have found out about the times they lived in. But I did not. I know almost nothing about them really. Their courtship? Working in the pits? The Lock-out in the Depression? Losing their second child? Being dusted as a miner? The shootings at Rothbury? My uncles killed in the War? Love on the dole? There were hundreds, thousands of questions that I would now like to ask them. But, alas, I can't. It's too late.

Thus, prompted by my guilt, I resolved to write these books. They describe happenings that affected people, real people. The whole series is, to coin a modern phrase, designed to push your buttons, to make you remember and wonder at things forgotten. The books might just let nostalgia see the light of day, so that oldies and youngies will talk about the past and re-discover a heritage otherwise forgotten. Hopefully, they will spark discussions between generations, and foster the asking and answering of questions that should not remain unanswered.

BORN IN 1943?
WHAT ELSE HAPPENED

RON WILLIAMS

BOOK 5 IN A SERIES OF 35
FROM 1939 TO 1973

BOOM BOOKS

BOOM, BOOM BABY, BOOM

BORN IN 1943? WHAT ELSE HAPPENED?

Published by Boom Books
Wickham, NSW, Australia
Web: boombooks.biz
Email: email@boombooks.biz

© Ron Williams 2012. This printing 2023.

ISBN: 9780987543608 (Paperback)
Australia--History--Miscellanea--20th century.

Cover images: National Archives of Australia.

A11663, PA189 Sweethearts take a break from war;

M3130, 157 Eileen Lenihan OBE, PM's Private Secretary;

A11663, PA189 Italian POWs arriving in Oz;

MP1113/1, 319 Bofors Volunteer Defence Corps at Newcastle, NSW.

TABLE OF CONTENTS

IMPORTANT PEOPLE AND EVENTS

King of England	George VI
Prime Minister of Australia	John Curtin
Leader of Opposition	Arthur Fadden
Governor General	Baron Gowrie
Pope	Pius XII
US President	Franklin Roosevelt
PM of Britain	Winston Churchill
Emperor of Japan	Hirohito

WINNER OF THE ASHES

1938	Draw, 1 - all
1939- 45	WWII. No play
1946 - 47	Australia 3 - 0

MELBOURNE CUP WINNERS

1942	Felonius
1943	Dark Felt
1944	Sirius

ACADEMY AWARDS 1943

Best Actor	James Cagney
Best Actress	Greer Garson
Best Movie	Mrs Minerva

INTRODUCTION TO THE SERIES

I was five years old when the War started. But even at that early age, I was aware of the dread, and yet excitement, that such an epoch-making event brought to my small coal-mining town. At the start, it was not at all certain that it would affect us at all, but quickly it became obvious that everybody in the nation would become seriously involved in it. The most immediate response I remember was that all the Mums (who still remembered WWI) were worried that their sons and husbands would be taken away and killed. After that, I can remember radio speeches given by Chamberlain, Churchill, Lyons, Menzies, and Curtin telling of hard times ahead, but promising certain victory over our wicked foes.

For a young boy, as the War years went on, reality and fantasy went hand in hand. As I heard of our victories, I day-dreamed of being at the head of our Military forces, throwing grenades and leading bayonet charges. I sank dozens of battleships from my submarine that was always under attack. And I lost count of the squadrons of Messerschmitts that I sent spiraling from the sky. Needless to say, I was awarded a lot of medals and, as I got a bit older, earned the plaudits of quite a few pretty girls.

But, mixed in with all this romance, were some more analytical thoughts. Every day, once the battles got going, I would go to the newspapers' maps of where the battlelines currently were. One for the Western front, one in North Africa, and a third in Russia. Later, another in the Pacific. Then I would examine them minutely to see just how far we had moved, backwards or forward. I read all the reports, true and false, and gloated when it was said we were winning, and shrunk away at our losses.

At the personal level, I remember the excitement of getting up at 4am on a few days when nearby Newcastle was under submarine attack. We went to our underground air-raid shelter that we shared with a neighbour, and listened, and occasionally looked out, for some who-knows-what enemies to appear. It really was a bit scary. I can remember too the brown-outs, and the black-outs, the searchlights, the tank-traps, the clackers that were given to wardens to warn of gas attacks, and the gasmasks that 20 town-wardens carried, presumably to save a town of 2,000 people when needed. There was the rationing, the shortages of everything, and even the very short shirt tails that a perceptive Government decreed were necessary to win the War.

At the start of researching this book, everything started to come back to me. Things such as those above, and locations like Dunkirk, Tobruk, El Alamain, Stalingrad, and Normandy. Really, at this stage these names kept popping up, but I was at loss as to how significant they were. Also, names of people. Hitler and Mussolini I knew were baddies. But **how** bad? Chamberlain was always criticised for his appeasement, but what were his alternatives? Who **were** Ribbentrop and Molotov, and Tojo and Blamey, and what was Vichy France?

And finally, when war did come, and grind on, year after year, what effect did it have back here in Australia? How did we as a society cope with a world that just had to continue on, given that the sons and dads of the nation were actually being killed daily overseas? When the postman did his normal delivery and brought a letter saying your loved one is dead? What did we do when old jobs suddenly disappeared, and new ones were created a hundred miles away? When goods, always readily available, were no longer for sale? When everything changed?

It was all a hotch-potch to me when I started this series. At the end of it, I can say it is a lot clearer. I have sorted out the countable things like battles, locations, people, and rules and regulations. I can appreciate, too, the effects on society, though these can only be ascertained from what I **have** researched, and make no allowance for all that I have missed.

In presenting this book, I have started every Chapter with a look at the military events in the world, often with the Pacific first , then Europe and the Middle East. Then I come back to Oz to see how we are faring in a military sense within the nation. After that, I blunder about reporting and speculating on which aspects of life here were affected by these, and other ongoing, matters.

So, despite all the talk about the War above, and despite the fact that it was the controlling influence on all of our lives, the **thrust of these books is about the social changes and** reactions that took place in this period, **here in Oz**.

AUSTRALIA'S LEGACY FROM 1942

The domestic scene. Australia was frightened and bewildered. 1942 had been a dreadful year, the worst the nation had ever seen. It started with the Japanese coming at the nation from all directions, blasting their way through all the little and big nations and islands around the western

Pacific, everywhere from the Philippines to Burma. Island after island fell in December 1942, and then a few months later the lands of what is now Indonesia progressively succumbed. Then came Allied defeats in Malaya and the supposed impregnable bastion of Singapore, followed by Japanese landings in northern and eastern New Guinea, and it seemed to Australians that the yellow peril could never be turned away.

This was not all. In the middle of the year, the Japs got three midget submarines into Sydney Harbour, and they fired off a few shells before being sunk. Sydney and Newcastle were shelled from the sea, and a dozen freighters were sunk off the NSW coast. Darwin was bombed in March, and the deaths there were greater than at Pearl Harbour. It was also attacked repeatedly throughout the rest of the year, and so too were Broome and small cities on the east coast of far north Queensland.

The nation's response to these terrible months. Every citizen had the same two responses to this situation. **The first response** was to ask themselves, and sometimes others, whether the Japs would continue their thrust southward until all of Australia was under its flag. In public, some brave souls pooh-pahed this idea, arguing that there was no economic or military benefit for the Japs if they did so. Others said that they might occupy only the north of the country in the first years, and slowly conquer the vast territories of Australia at a more leisurely pace later. The really brave souls were the many who said that someone, perhaps the Brits or the Americans, would come to our rescue. These people were brave because, as far as the

Brits were concerned, they clearly were not interested in helping Australia until the War in Europe was over. And the Americans, when they did intervene on our behalf, did so only because we provided good bases for their counter-attacks on the Japanese. At June, 1942, realists were pretty sure that Oz was friendless and doomed. Even though very few of them said this out loud.

The second response was a feeling of immense and over-whelming sorrow for the men, young and old, who were suffering the horrors of war with the Japanese. Over 15,000 men were captured as Singapore fell, and the ones who survived spent the rest of the War in Jap prison camps like Changi. Thousands and thousands of others were killed, or maimed, or psychologically destroyed in action in a dozen different countries. Every day, the newspapers would carry a listing of the dead and wounded and missing, and every day a hundred families would get the dreaded letter from the postman saying that their son, their brother, their father, was dead or might never return.

The population responded as best it could. Every thing was different. Men up to forty years either volunteered or were drafted to the armed Services. Many women were called upon to take the jobs that men had vacated, and lots of these found themselves in munitions and arms factories, working 60 hours a week. Every one was severely rationed, and coupons were needed to buy clothes butter, tea and petrol, and other stuff. Everything was scarce, and some of it was obtainable only on the black market. The wise Government also placed restrictions on the production of thousands of so-called luxury items, so that they could not be bought.

Pink icing for cakes was forbidden, though white icing was not. The tails of men's shirts were shortened to the level just below the waist, and men's suits were available only in three styles that the Government fancied. Waistcoats were forbidden.

The Government interfered in the control of the War news and general societal news. Their excuse was that unrestricted news services would provide valuable information to the enemy, and that, at the street level, "careless talk costs lives". Of course they were right, but they carried it much too far. People with sons fighting overseas had the right to as much information as possible, and **not the bare minimum that the machine allowed**. Time and again throughout 1942, the bumbling secrecy aroused public antipathy, and then a re-organisation of the censorship bureaucracy would occur. But undeterred, these enthusiasts for secrecy soldiered on, and their excesses continued into 1943.

Overall, the Australian community responded very well to all the new pressures they felt. No one liked the rationing, and there were endless complaints about it. But everyone could see that there was a good reason for it, and took it in their stride. The same was true for compulsory military service, and all the other rules and regulations that were introduced. The fact was that the people of the nation were, for a half year, scared stiff, and were prepared to make all sorts of sacrifices if they seemed likely to keep the Japs away from our shores.

OZ POLITICS IN 1942

The Prime Minister at this time was Labour's **John Curtin**. He was widely respected by all sides of politics, and ruled the Labour Party without challenge. Like everyone else in Oz at the time, he could hardly keep up with the ever-changing situation in the nation, but he did his very best and that turned out to be good enough.

He had, however, one major fight that went on for all of the year, and beyond. That was with Britain's Prime Minister, Winston Churchill, and to a smaller extent, President Roosevelt of the USA. Churchill had a set of priorities that were different form Curtin's. He thought that the **war in Europe** was the top priority, and that every thing else was subordinate to that. In practice, this meant that all the resources of war should be **concentrated in England** and the European sphere, and that Empire countries like Australia **were expendable at the moment**, and could be won back from the enemy after Hitler had been beaten.

John Curtin thought differently. He was Prime Minister of **Australia**, and thought that our troops already in Britain and the Middle East should be repatriated as soon as possible. He also thought that Britain should send planes and troops and armaments to Australia in the same time frame. After all, he reasoned, in **WWI** Australia had rushed troops to Britain. Then for the **first two years of WWII**, we had done the same. We had suffered greatly in Tobruk, and lost thousands of men by Churchill's ineptitude in Greece and Crete. We had even lost more men **defending British oil interests** in the Middle East. **Now**, Curtin urged, **was the time** for Britain to honour its assumed promise, and send us the help we needed.

Churchill reluctantly and slowly sent home some of our troops, but no **British** manpower, and little else. The British fortress at Singapore, that had promised to somehow control the Pacific, fell only a few months after the Pacific war started, and was of no use to us. So the two Prime Ministers battled it out for all of 1942. **Churchill was determined to defend British interests at all costs, and Curtin was equally determined to defend Australia's.**

The other major political problem for the Government was the **call for a National Government.** This meant that, for the War period, instead of having the Labour Party in power harassed by a United Party Opposition, the two parties should bury their differences and pull together in a combined single government. This was what Britain had done, and it was working well enough.

Here, though, Labour was reluctant to hand over some of its power to the Opposition, and was adamant in its refusal to do so. This was a pity, because it was obvious to all that some Labour Ministers were quite **out of their depth and thoroughly power-crazed**, and that there were better men in the Opposition who could take their place. Still, Curtin and his merry men stood firm, and the two-party system remained firmly in place, despite non-stop pleas from everywhere to scrap it for the while.

AMERICA AND AUSTRALIA 1942

Hitler's first big mistake of the War was to invade Russia. Up till 1941, Germany had appeared to be co-existing with Russia, and indeed both nations had been trading in war materials very comfortably. Then Hitler suddenly invaded Russia, but after about a year of successes, was now slowly being forced back towards his own borders. This **eastern**

war was sapping Germany's energies, and was costing far more resources than he could afford.

Hitler's second big mistake was to declare War on America after the Japs attacked Pearl Harbour. America retaliated on Hitler, and thus became committed to involvement in the European War. If Hitler had simply held his tongue, America would probably not have become thus committed, and Hitler's chances of success would have been sky high.

Roosevelt was suddenly thrust into a war on two fronts. **His interests were entirely those of America.** In particular, in our sphere, he wanted to beat the Japs. If he could help Australia on the way, that was a good thing. **But that was not his aim.** His Supreme Commander in the Pacific, General MacArthur, who came to Australia about the middle of 1942, was even more definite and outspoken on this matter than Roosevelt, and Curtin was left in **no doubt that the Americans were here to further America's aims, and only for that purpose.**

THE SECOND HALF ON 1942

The arrogant and publicity–hungry **MacArthur** set up head-quarters in Brisbane, and from mid- year, the number of American bases in north Queensland, and elsewhere, increased rapidly. The Americans took to the skies, and suddenly the combined Air Forces of the two nations were able to turn the tables on the Japanese. **We were able to bomb their bases.**

On top of that, the US fleets had two notable victories in the Coral Sea and in the Solomons. Australians in New Guinea pushed the Japs back into the sea as they tried to conquer New Guinea from the north. An attempted landing at Milne Bay was fought off by Oz troops. In the last **six months of the year, the Japanese learned they were not invincible,** that their navy, their air force and their army could be defeated. They also realised, **by Christmas**, that whatever **plans they had, to capture Australia, were to no avail,** and that they could no longer hope to do so.

Australians in these months felt that the situation was improving. Of course, **censorship** was very much still in evidence, so news that was published about our success was greatly delayed and couched in officialese. Still, the news **did** get through, and the mood of the nation lightened as it did. By the end of the year, most people thought that the emergency had gone away. John Curtin did not acknowledge this, because **he wanted Oz to remain on a full war footing.** But the population did come to know, and many a person slept sounder at Christmas than they did in mid-June.

One thing, however, still haunted a million people. The thought that their men-folk were still out there, somewhere, fighting for their country. Every day still they dreaded the news that the postman might bring. It was terrible thought, mixed in with the glee that the nation was safe, but that **their loved ones were not.**

THE WAR IN EUROPE.

Britain had seen the worst of its War. She had declared war on Germany after that nation had invaded Poland in 1939. Over the next year, she had seen her own troops beaten in Norway, and then humiliated in France (at Dunkirk). She had suffered the terrors of air-bombing in the Battle of

Britain for five months. Her Empire troops had suffered huge losses in north Africa, and also in Greece and Crete.

In the skies, she had gone from dubious equality to a position of superiority where she was now **sending large bombing forces nightly to occupied German cities, and even to Italy.**

Her Navy has suffered terribly. Her above-surface fleet had always more than performed well. But the German submarines, especially in 1942, had been taking a severe toll on merchant vessels. Their subs had travelled world wide, and turned up in South America and even to the south of Australia. Now, at the end of 1942, this situation seemed to be a bit better than it had been, and maybe the Battle of the Atlantic might be coming to an end.

So Britain was completely free from thoughts of invasion. It was also watching with some glee the slaughter that was taking place on the Eastern front between the forces of Russia and Germany. While **Joseph Stalin's** Russia was holding the Germans at bay, Britain could breathe easy. In fact, she was now sending large resources to her Russian ally, such as the 500 fighter planes that Churchill had originally scheduled for Australia.

In north Africa, the battles were nearly over. The sole place where the Nazis were still fighting was in Tunisia, and they would be cleaned-out fully by June 1943. So Britain could begin **talking** about starting a Second Front, which meant that she might invade some part of German-occupied Europe, and march towards Germany. Of course, in 1943, she had no intention of **doing** this, but the besieged Russians were anxious for some relief and talk of this Second Front kept them hopeful and willing to keep fighting.

Let me add, in case I have not made it clear, that Churchill and his Ministers and the centre of power, Whitehall, made no mention at all of sending aid to Australia, and had no intention of doing so in the near future.

MY RULES IN WRITING

Note. In this book, I rely a lot on re-producing **Letters from the newspapers**. When I do this, I put the text in a different font, and indent it a little, and make the font somewhat smaller. I do not edit the text at all. That is, I do not correct spelling or grammar, and if the text gets garbled, I do not correct it. It's just as it was seen in the Papers.

Second note. The material for this book, when it comes from newspapers, is reported as it was seen at the time. If the benefit of hindsight over the years changes things, then I might record that in my Comments. The info reported thus reflects matters as they were seen in 1943.

Third note. Let me also apologise in advance to anyone I might offend. In a work such as this, **it is certain some people will think I got some things wrong. I am sure that I did,** but please remember, **all of this is only my opinion**. And really, my opinion does not matter one little bit in the scheme of things. **I hope you will say "silly old bugger"**, and shrug your shoulders and read on.

So, now, strap yourself in, and we will go out together and finish these Wars in a few easy months. The boys should be back home for Christmas.

JANUARY NEWS ITEMS

The Queen's New Years Honours list usually distributes honours to men and women from all walks of life. **This year** it was restricted to **members of the Armed Services**.

News report. Typical examples of war-time exaggeration and propaganda: "In the early morning of December 20, for six hours, 20 AIF Commandos in Portuguese Timor fought off 500 Japanese who were storming the aerodrome, and **for the loss of three men, they killed at least 100 Japanese**".

News report from January 1st. Although the **Federal Government** has ordered **that today should be observed as a normal working day**, statements made yesterday alleged that thousands of workers would be absent from their jobs today.

The Federal Government today added more items to **its existing very, very long list of prohibited items**. These included: bitters, aerated and mineral waters; dates; infants and invalid foods; mustard seed, dried vegetables; tapestries, velvet velveteens, trimmings, tinsel belting; bath mats; food choppers; music stools and table screws; sporting guns and rifles; metal pins in fancy boxes; pens and pencils in fancy boxes;oiled silks and piece goods for parasols.

News item from January 2nd. Government factories said that **35,000 employees did not turn up for work on New Years Day**. Their reason was that the Government refused to pay them double time for the shift. Dr Evatt, the Attorney General, stated that prosecutions would be launched against many of those who did not front for work.

The Director-General of Manpower said that in future **an order restricting the employment of domestic servants would apply to all** of NSW. Previously domestic servants were employed by many households. Much hardship is expected among the elderly and sick.

News item January 8th. **Seventy-seven men were charged in Court with failing to report for work on New Year's Day.** They were placed on a good-behavior bond requiring that they report for work in future. The cases against a further 160 men will be held over the next few days.

Sugar was tightly rationed. However, the Minister for Trade and Customs announced that an **extra six pounds per person** for the purpose of **jam-making** would be made.

It seems likely that the Federal Government will introduce **a new system of collecting income tax.** The existing system was to base tax for next year on **your income from last year**, and the tax was paid in a few lump sums throughout the year. It is now suggesting that **a pay-as-you-go** system will be introduced, under which taxation will be deducted each fortnight from the wages actually earned in that fortnight. Sounds messy, and has obvious flaws.

Under National Security Regulations most **strikes were illegal.** At mid-January, 100 workers at Millford

Colliery had a few stoppages in one week, and now were issued with summonses. The Regulation banning strikes **was about to be tested in Court.**

Public holidays. The Government announced that persons not engaged in war production **will be allowed a holiday** on up-coming Australia Day. **Essential workers would be paid at their normal penalty rates. Old Governments can learn new tricks.**

An Australia-wide order limiting the speed of motor vehicles to **40 m.p.h.** (60 km per hour) has been announced by the Land Transport Board, to operate from February 1. It will apply to **all** Australia, including **the country and the outback**. The aim is to preserve petrol, and be the subject of ridicule.

The Japs are still out there. MacArthur announced that a **Japanese submarine had sunk an Australian vessel** off **the east coast** of Oz. The crew was rescued, but there was little further detail.

Several large Trade Unions in Newcastle **will strike from tomorrow unless pubs make schooner glasses available** before 4pm. Schooners are less profitable to pub-owners than are smaller glasses, and owners are currently restricting their use for a large part of the day. The Unions involved include Watersiders, Moulders, Bricklayers and Gas Employees.

The Minister for the Army defended the actions of the Army in prosecuting **a soldier's mother** for having **harboured her son** while he was absent without leave. **Would you?**

JANUARY: OZ NOT ON HOLIDAYS

Under normal conditions, prior to the Pacific War, Australia just about stopped doing anything in the New Year. Families packed up and went somewhere else, for a few weeks. Half the population headed for the North or South Coast into holiday shacks, caravans, or tents. Of the rest, city dwellers travelling to the country passed the yokels going to the city. Most people had some favourite spot to go to, and went there year after year. Once they got there, they relaxed. Swimming, and slothing, and eating and drinking, they forgot about the worries of the world, forgot about newspapers, and re-charged their batteries for the year ahead.

Lucky Australia? Normally. But not this year. There was none of that. There was a war on, and guns and munitions were needed, roads and airfields had to be built, coal and shipping and food were needed in large quantities. This meant that everyone had to stay with their noses to the grindstone, and work their normal shift, probably plus overtime. So the Government enforced **regulations that forbade citizens from taking their holidays in January.** If there were some people, say the self-employed, who escaped these regulations, then public pressure forced then to conform. How could they stop producing when the boys in the trenches were doing it so tough?

The Letters to the *SMH* clearly reflected this situation. The usual pattern was that in **January**, Letters were about trivia or minor irritations, like the fly-covers being left off the jugs they left out for the milkman. Lots of them were deliberately capricious, and waves of them followed some idiotic theme, such as the making of bread from sea-weed.

Not so this year. **There was no frivolity at all**. People were not in a holiday mood. Their Letters were deadly serious, and about heavy themes. The writers were tired, over-worked, run-down, and exasperated but, at the same time, they produced Letters that were better-written and more logical than in any other month that I have seen in writing all my books.

Comment. It seems to me that **everyone was really shocked** when January came and there was no break from work. Serious men and women from all over the place seriously took stock of the situation. On the face of it, they knew that the dangers of invasion had receded, though our men-folk in the Armed Forces were still at risk. They also appreciated that the war-effort had to continue, and that **now** was not the time to slacken off. Yet, given the improved military situation, they were quickly realising that **many of the regulations** imposed on them had been unnecessary. They looked at the **Government muddling** that everyone could see round them every day, they looked at the **failure of Government man-power management** that everyone had experienced, they looked at the structure of Parliament and knew that many of the Labour Ministers, **who were exercising so much power, were not worth feeding.**

So contemplative writers round the country, doubtless stung by their denial of a New Year's break, sat down and wrote serious Letters attacking all aspects of Government. These were not just Letters to the *Sydney Morning Herald*, but Letters to all the major dailies across the nation.

Over the next few pages, I will present a few samples of these.

JOHN CURTIN AND HIS LABOUR MINISTRY

The Labour Party was adamant that they would not share power with the United Party. Some of the opposition to sharing came from existing Government **ministers,** who thought they might lose their jobs. Could, for example, Doc Evatt, the current erratic Attorney General, withstand a challenge from Bob Menzies, with his careful, well-thought-out policies? Could Arthur Calwell and Eddie Ward, both volatile gentlemen, hold their spots. The existing Minister for Creating Shortages and Spreading Misery, John Dedman, might get toppled. None of these would support **any** thought of a National Government. On top of that, the Trade Unions generally opposed such, and that added nails to its coffin.

In any case, in the next few Letters, John Curtin was roundly attacked over this matter, and other perceived faults. Note, however, that the writers were rather kind to him as a person, even though they attacked his policies. Curtin himself continued to hold the respect of the nation.

Letters, Arthur Bailey. The Prime Minister's New Year message demands that we be bigger Australians in every way. Had he spoken thus as the head of a **National** Government, it would have sounded as a clarion call to the nation instead of being merely **a message from the head of a party** which gets little support from its own followers, judging by their disobedience over working on New Years' Day and their small per capita **subscriptions to war loans**. Let Mr Curtin lead the way by being a big Australian himself, and unite the nation with a Government of the best qualities in all parties.

Letters, A de R Barclay. Since he has been in office, during the most difficult period in the history of Australia, Mr Curtin has shown certain qualities of statesmanship that lift him above the common level of his party. There can be no doubt, therefore, that the humiliation to which his party has put him recently must have convinced him of the rottenness of the system that made that humiliation possible. This is no time for party, but a time for whole-souled national effort. How can the making of that effort be assured while that despicable thing, party interest, is allowed to discolour **the pure stream of patriotism?** How is it possible, without the establishment of a truly National Government, composed of men of single purpose and divorced from party ties?

Letters, Australian. In urging the early formation of a National government, Col K Martin voices an opinion that is daily gaining adherents throughout the community. Recent events have emphasised the extent to which Mr Curtin is and can be hampered in the prosecution of the war by forces whose vision is distorted by party interest, and whose allegiance is rather to a so-called policy than to the cause of national survival, which is, after all, what we are fighting for. If we lose the war, there will be no place in Australia for an ALP or any other sectional organisation.

Whether Mr Curtin goes to America to confer with Mr Roosevelt or not, he should speedily free himself from the hampering ties that bind him, purge his Cabinet of those influences that are so obviously making his hard task harder, and **make his Government representative of the best brains and best will available.** If he did that he would increase his own stature and strengthen

Australia's position in a time of real and unprecedented national peril.

Letters, Abe Turner. I hurts me a great deal to have to criticise the Labour Party, which I have supported all my life. But to see Curtin bullied and fooled by his Ministers leaves me no choice.

Those ministers are complete bullies who are telling the nation that they have **some great mission to save the nation**, and that all their rules and regulations are necessary. Most of them are not. These Ministers, and their always-growing bureaucracies that they have surrounded themselves with, are completely at odds with what is really needed. That is thoughtful consideration of Australia's needs, and thoughtful plans executed to fix whatever is up.

Half of these ministers are **really trying to introduce socialism by stealth, using the war as an excuse.** Most of the others are so personally ambitious, **and get their credits from issuing a daily list of imperatives**, without even an hour's consideration.

I know Mr Curtin has **only the smallest majority in Parliament, and so he is unwilling to rock the boat.** But I can assure him that if he does sack these men, the electorate will first of all rejoice, and then support him all the way. A National government of all Parties could then be created, and Labour would again be fulfilling what are clearly the nation's wishes.

Comment. It was a war-time fact that people realised that **to question too loudly the policies** being pursued by the Government **could result in action being taken against you**. You might keep this in mind as you consider the above Letters and the subsequent sets. Mr Turner above must have been fairly close to the wind. So too might have been the *SMH* for publishing that Letter.

EXCESSIVE RULES AND REGULATIONS

On January 20th, a special report in the *SMH* said that, **since the start of the Pacific War**, the Federal Government had introduced 820 Statutes embracing **2,350 Regulations**. It had opened 14 extra new Departments, and employed an extra 1,000 in its bureaucracy. All of these were under the National Security Act. As well as this, **other Acts and Departments had more than doubled the number of Regulations, and the States had thoroughly enjoyed similar involvements.**

For example, the NSW Government controlled matters such as black-outs and brown-outs at night, street lighting, and the lighting for cars. It said that race meetings could be held on only **some** Saturdays, air-raid shelters must be built by certain businesses and people, that slit-trenches must be provided in some areas, that rents and prices of meat and other goods were fixed, and that certain vegetables and fruits could or could not be grown by farmers. The list of restraints on personal freedom went on and on, and as people got more familiar with the idea that the Japs had gone away, they got more vocal in wanting the sillier regulations to be lifted.

The *SMH*, in its usual measured way, got the ball rolling.

SMH editorial. Unquestionably the intervention of Parliament has become necessary to check the activities of certain Ministers, whose political bias tempts them to issue regulations serving no obvious war purpose, and having a **predominant party flavor.**

There has not been time for the usual peace-time procedure of the review by Parliament of new laws, or for the testing of their validity in the Courts. Indeed, some of them would probably not survive legal challenge. Yet from most of the new restrictions there is **no appeal**, save to some departmental authority. It is obviously improper that this hurriedly augmented bureaucracy should usurp the functions of both the Legislature and of the Judiciary.

Letters, Telford Simpson. In time of war, a Government has to be given plenary powers, at any rate so far as essential matters are concerned; but the National Security Act and the regulations made thereunder are so wide that many injustices and irritations are caused to the public in the name of national security that might well be avoided in the national interest. Some of these injustices and irritations do not even come within the wide ambit of the National Security Act. The Act gives opportunity to Ministers and officials who have some pet theory of their own to implement it by regulation, even **though such a theory can only be remotely connected with the national security.**

The Proprietary Medicines Regulations, for example, provide not only that all **secret** formulae should be disclosed to the authorities, but also all such information as is necessary to enable the medicine to be manufactured and the rights of the owner to be defeated. It places a prohibition on advertising, production, and distribution of patent medicines, at the whim of the Minister. It would, I suggest, be stretching the words "national security" beyond their reasonable limits to be able to include such a regulation within their meaning. It is, I suggest, impossible to justify the forced disclosure of such a nature on the ground of national security.

Letters, B Walters. May I suggest some steps which should be taken to check bureaucracy?

One. Every elector should write to his Federal member warning him that unless he protests in the House against the folly of needlessly irritating the public for no useful war purpose, as Mr Dedman's Department and some Army officials are doing at present, the elector will vote against him at the next elections.

Two. Protest meetings should be organised in the Town Hall and all large provincial centres, from which resolutions should be sent to the Prime Minister.

Three. A Citizens' Protection League should be formed which should exercise the utmost vigilance in respect of the swarm of new regulations which are being almost daily foisted upon an all too indifferent public. Opposition should be aroused to such absurdities as sending able-bodied young men (who should be in the Army), to dressmakers' establishments, in order to inspect the width of the seam of women's skirts.

Letters, W Francis. Since the war began 830 sets of regulations and 2,400 proclamations under the National Security Act have been gazetted. These regulations and proclamations cover a wide field of human activity.

They delegate, to a large number of Civil Servants by name, the powers of the Ministers of State over whose names the proclamations appear in official print. Many of these orders have no relation to national security, and some indeed may hinder the war effort. But they all have one common feature. They transfer control of private life and affairs from the citizen to Ministers and their army of delegates. In other words, they destroy the very basis of democracy, and create a state of bureaucratic socialism, regardless of the will of the people.

In the meantime, Government Departments are increasing in number and size, **the printing and filling in of forms goes on and on**, and countless hours are wasted daily by the people in desperate attempts to conform to the multitude of demands and restrictions. What cumulative effect the innumerable irritations and delays and the sense of frustration must have on the effort and spirit of a country at war is beyond calculation.

Letters, R Simpson. The Government is calling upon all owners of "electricity generators" to supply particulars. "Machines used or capable of being used as generators of electricity" (in the words of the notice) are exceedingly numerous and of many types. Presumably, though it is not so stated, only electro-magnetic machines are meant, but, even so, the range is extremely wide. Practically all electric motors, whether for direct or alternating current, and down to the smallest sizes, are "capable of being used for the generation of electricity,"

Does the Government really want to be overwhelmed with full details of all the electric motors, even including toys, in the country? If not, why not get someone who knows something about the subject to draw up the notice?

A SORRY STORY FROM BROOME

On January 19th, the Oz Government revealed that, on March 3rd **last year**, Broome harbour was attacked by Japanese fighters. The harbour was dotted with 15 or more Catalina seaplanes and the like, and most of them were filled with women and children who were due to be returned to their homeland in the Dutch Indies.

All 15 of them were sunk, and the passengers were mainly killed, as were many of the crews. The harbour was without defences, so all Japanese planes returned safely to their base. The town itself was not attacked.

This sad news was deeply felt by the nation. However, much of the sadness turned to anger when it was realised that the Government had **sat on this information for 10 months.** There could be no reason for this, given that obviously the Japanese knew all about it. Whatever the reason might have been, it was clear that it was the Government's view that the nation could not be trusted with the truth. It had to be fed all the good stories, exaggerated to unbelievable proportions, and every now and then given some small snippet of bad, real, news that Government could not continue to suppress.

For example, every day in January, the papers were filled with success stories. Both in the Pacific and Europe, Allied planes bombed enemy cities and bases, and typical press reports of the raids said we shot down 40 enemy planes and lost only 4. In ground fighting and in submarines, the figures were **equally unbelievable. Given this delayed news from Broome, who would believe the official news in future?** Perhaps the Government was delaying **lots** of current news for some internal political reason. Everyone knew that they could get really **up-to-date news from Lord Haw Haw in Germany and Tokyo Rose in Japan, simply by using their short wave radios.** Why not do that?

The upshot was that censorship bureaus lost even more face with the public. And so too did all those who were pushing **the fatuous lines of deceit and concealment.**

Letters, Anti-Humbug. Mr Curtin says the bombing of Broome should be a lesson to us. It is a lesson – but not as Mr Curtin expects. It is an exposure of the senseless strangling power of censorship, and we are filled with doubt and suspicion. What other disasters have happened within the last nine months and of which we have never been informed?

Letters, D A K. Does hush-hush pay, or what purpose does it achieve? For some time the public has been fed on the theory that it is unwise to disclose losses or gains, in order that the enemy should not be informed of results. To given the Jap his due, he is not a nit-wit, and Japanese bomber crews knew at once what they had achieved in the open spaces of Broome.

Perhaps if the voters made the members of Parliament feel that they must insist upon speedy and accurate information upon such matters as "the Broome story", then the people would be alive to the danger at our very doors.

Letters, J, Pymble. The belated Press reports say that on the day previous to the raid six Japanese reconnaissance planes surveyed the spot. If this is correct, one wonders why the planes located at Broome were not promptly removed, or at least the passengers removed, to a place of safety instead of being left in the open for the raid that could only be expected when it was known the Japanese had discovered such an easy unprotected target. Was this lesson taken?

Comment. These were not just the views of a few. **Distrust of our propaganda was widespread and long-lasting.**

FEBRUARY NEWS ITEMS

Australia has completed the manufacture of its **first Beaufort Torpedo bomber, from drawing-board to test-flight.** This was done in just two years, and was faster than similar times in US, Britain, and Canada.

Tank experts who saw **Australian-designed tanks** undergoing their acceptance tests in NSW yesterday said they were the fastest tanks of their weight in the world.

The Deputy Director of Man-power said that **2,000 carpenters** were wanted for works of the highest priority.

18,000 carpenters will be required to fill in forms indicating what work they are currently employed in doing. These forms will be assessed by Officers who will determine if **their current job is essential for the war effort.** If it is not, **they will be drafted** to do more productive work somewhere in Australia.

In NSW, **school-children**, whether accompanied by parents or not, will not be allowed in future to travel **on the upper decks of buses** in peak traffic hours unless the full adult fare is paid.

The Minister for Munitions said in the House of Representatives that **production of munitions was now more than the Army could absorb.** "For example, we have **over-capacity for making .303 bullets.**"

Mr Jack Oppy, of Condobolin, has just had returned to him **a message** which he placed **in a bottle** and threw into the sea **27 years ago.**

New taxation scales will apply from April 1st. Tax will start at $104 per year, instead of the current $156. Tax at that rate will be sixpence in the Pound, and will rise to **eighteen shillings and sixpence** at an income of five thousand Pounds.

Sydney's majestic Markus Clark building has been granted to the military for **a services hostel**. Work on the change-over is nearing completion. Similar events happened in all States.

Defence authorities have decided that **headlamp masks may be removed** from cars in all locations south of Rockhampton.

Steps have been taken by the **Dept of War Organisation** to increase the production of **perambulators**, for which demand had been heavy. Mr Dedman, the Minister, has arranged for the release of materials, and the manufacture of **a** design which has been agreed upon by the Baby Welfare Department, and representatives of mothers' organisations.

A meeting of **1,500 members** of the Amalgamated Engineering Union in Sydney Town Hall decided to strike if the Women's Employees Board **did not grant equal pay for women** in the industry.

India's Ghandi was on **another hunger strike** against the British Government's refusal to grant independence to India. He was being held as a prisoner at the Viceroy's palace. His condition, as reported on February 27th , was "very grave". He has now been fasting for 17 days, and is scheduled to continue for another 4 days.

HOW IS THE WAR GOING?

Every day the *SMH* provided a **summary** of what was happening in **each of the main theatres of the War**. Right throughout January, and February as well, the reports had been thoroughly favourable. Below, **I have taken a single day**, and reported the summary verbatim.

The Russians have achieved outstanding success by capturing the great German base at Kursk, 130 miles west of Voronej and about 90 miles south of Orel. The Soviet force which previously cut the highroad between Kursk and Orel made a flank attack from the north-west to assist the main Russian assault on the city.

Berlin Radio has announced that the complete evacuation of the Lorient district by today has been ordered. Lorient, on the French Atlantic coast, is one of Germany's key submarine bases. On Sunday night it received its heaviest attack from two waves of RAF bombers.

Moscow Radio quotes a Berne (Switzerland) report that troops have been sent to Genoa, Naples, Turin, Milan (all of which have suffered severely from RAF raids), and Rome to prevent mass action against the Italian Government. Naples port was blasted in daylight on Sunday by two waves of US Liberator bombers.

Copenhagen, Danish capital, and home of the world's greatest Diesel engine plant, vital to German U-boat construction, was bombed three times on Monday night, according to the Malmo (25 miles from Copenhagen) correspondent of the Stockholm "Tidningen."

Guadalcanal Evacuated. – Japan admits that Guadalcanal has been evacuated.

Tokyo Radio states that the Japanese lost 15,743 killed or dead through illness, and 17 aircraft in New Guinea and Guadalcanal.

Air Raid in North. – When Australian and Dutch aircraft raided the Dutch-occupied port of Dobo, in the Aru Islands (Arafura Sea), north of Australia, they dropped nine tons of bombs, and caused great devastation.

Photographs brought back by the crews show that, as the result of this and earlier raids, at least three-quarters of the town has been burnt out or leveled.

Tunisian Activity. – Guns of the British Eighth Army are believed to be shelling the first outposts of the Mareth line in Tunisia. These are not far from the frontier, which is now all under the control of the Eighth Army.

Messina, terminus of the train ferry between the mainland of Italy and Sicily, was heavily bombed in daylight on Monday.

Comment. I can say a lot about these reports. You will agree with me that things were going well everywhere for the Allies. And that was true not just for a few days, but for the entire first two months of the year. Of course, everyone knew that these victories were being won at a terrible cost in human lives, and day-after-day **our losses were not being mentioned**, and our wins exaggerated. Still, it was quite clear that we were at last winning this part of the War, and hopefully this would continue. Fingers crossed.

Here in Australia, as every day passed, we could see that the Japanese were getting further and further from our shores. John Curtin and his friends had the impossible chore of **balancing** this good news with all sorts of admonitions that said we must keep our nose to the grindstone, that we needed more troops, that we should suffer all sorts of austerities ad infinitum so it seemed. Yet it was hard to argue **this** when the news from everywhere said it was time to relax.

The truth was that the Government was starting to lose its ability to influence some sections of the community. For example, about 12,000 teenagers left school at the end of 1942, and were required to register with Man-power authorities. But only 2,000 did so in the proper time-frame, and the authorities were having trouble sorting this out. In earlier months of the war, when people were told to register, they did so.

Another example, in January, the miners at a NSW colliery went on strike for a few days. There was much brave talk from the Government about how it had Emergency War-time powers to let hell loose on the strikers. But nothing of the sort happened. The miners were let off with a slap on the wrist, and it was plain to see that the Government and its agents were not ready for major industrial confrontation.

So, by the time February arrived, the mood of the nation had changed. People were questioning more and more what was the point of working themselves to exhaustion when the threat of invasion had gone? They had been working for about a year under harsh conditions as the Government and **employers took advantage of War-time patriotism to extract as much as possible from the work-force.** So, now, strikes flared up everywhere.

They were often sensible strikes, for reasonable conditions. **For example**, at the end of February 14,000 textile workers in Sydney factories struck to **have one week's annual leave**

inserted on their contract. **Then again**, coalminers in the
northern NSW field struck because they had been cajoled
into working abandoned and dangerous shafts to increase
the flow of war-time coal. **Now**, they sought to leave
these shafts, but were still being compelled to work them.
Remember too that Christmas and New Year had come
and gone, with the normal Christmas holiday abandoned.
And many workers had been punished for not working on
New Year's Day.

It was noticeable, at the same time when strikes were
abounding, that absenteeism was also on the rise. It all
pointed to a new mood that **workers were still prepared
to work hard if there was a reason for it, but if not, then
not**.

I should point out, though, that this was **not an attitude
universally held.** There were plenty of citizens who felt
that an all-out effort was still called for. I illustrate this with
a single Letter.

> **Letters, Camouflage Netter.** I protest against strikes
> that are occurring in many of our essential industries.
> We **camouflage netters**, all **working on a voluntary
> and unpaid basis,** and averaging 40 hours per week,
> feel that our fighting men are being sadly let down.
> We are giving up a great deal of our home life, and
> are saving the Government thousands of pounds. We
> appeal to Mr Curtin to adopt stronger measures to stop
> all strikes. We can only win this war if everyone puts
> his shoulder to the wheel and gives constant backing to
> our fighting forces everywhere.

CURTIN JUGGLES THE MILITIA

The Army in Oz was made up mainly of two parts. The **first** was called the **AIF**. It had been created in time for WWI, and carried through to the current time. The members of the force were long-term volunteers, and were now prepared to serve anywhere in the world. They were also quite committed to military life, and some of them were career soldiers. It was these men who over the last few years had won much glory in Tobruk, Greece and Crete.

The second part of the Army was called the **militia**. Over the last few years these units had gone through quite a few changes, but now were mainly **conscripted youths** who were called up for service around the time of their 18th birthday. They were thus mainly younger than members of the AIF, and less dedicated to the military. Having said that, it was these babies who had just turned back the Japanese as they tried to pass through Kokoda and capture southern New Guinea.

These two parts of the Army were not well disposed towards each other. One point of discord came from the fact that the AIF were expected to serve anywhere in the world, but the Militia was currently restricted to serve in Australia and its Territories. **This restriction** had been imposed on the Militia in WWI, and **was an integral part of Labour Party policy**. Right now, in February, this policy was under intense scrutiny from many sources, and it was John Curtin's role to find a compromise between the various protagonists.

His problem was basically that there were many people, both here and abroad, who reasoned that if we wanted US troops to come to Australia to defend us, then surely we should be prepared to send **all** of our troops to **anywhere** they were needed. But we were holding back half of our troops, the Militia, to defend solely our own shores. Curtin responded by defining an area that took in a bit more of the Pacific, from the 110th to the 159th Meridian and up to the Equator, and he said that our Militia could fight within those boundaries.

It was this proposal the eventually got Parliamentary approval.

But on the way, there was much said for and against sending our boys overseas. Many people argued that it made sense to keep a reserve on our continent in case the enemy came at us again. Others said that it made no difference because, in the broad scheme of things, we had so few troops that they made no difference. Of course, the criticism spread to other matters that were scarcely related to the real issue. In any case, the arguments waxed hot for the whole month, and Mr Curtin got quite a few references. I provide you with a sample.

Letters, Major J Shand, Legislative Assembly, Sydney. There should not be any limits set by Parliamentarians as to where our soldiers should be employed in combating the military power of nations who have plotted against the free democracies of the world for many years, and succeeded in temporarily occupying vital territory.

Letters, L Parker. Our present Government has more than once called aloud to the British and American Governments and armies, across the thousands of intervening oceanic miles, saying, in the historic Macedonian phrase, "Come over and help us." But even as we await expectantly a response to the latest of these supplications, this same Government, in a frame of mind strangely suggestive of dementia, enacts a law which says in effect, that no matter how generous that response may be, we on our part will so construct our army that it will be unable to do for them (or ourselves) what we have so urgently asked them to do for us.

This Government has undoubtedly done much to make a large proportion of the Australian people wince more or less painfully, but this latest action, both in the manner of its doing and its final and unfortunate consummation, seems to transcend all others in the effect on our national sensibilities.

Letters, E White. In these times, tolerance in our attitude to those from whom we differ is more than every necessary, but if the bill now before the House goes through in its present form Australia as a whole, the brave and the cowardly, the selfish and the unselfish may be branded as a nation of "squibs".

Letters, K McGregor, (ex 1ˢᵗ AIF). A number of your correspondents seem to possess no logical conception of Australia's military problem. Their letters on the Militia Bill contain too much emotion and not enough reason. With a total population of seven millions – which includes children, invalids, and the very old – **Australia has a definite limit to her effective manpower potential.** Experts alone could tell us just how many front-line troops we could muster, exclusive of ancillary units and lines of communication supports. We have but a limited supply of men for service in any part of the world. The bigger our army the more difficult becomes the question of reinforcement.

As I see it, the Curtin Government has wisely decided an area in which militiamen can serve at the present moment. The Government has refused to be stampeded into zoning the whole south-west Pacific as a base of operations for our man-power.

With the experience of the long, arduous and costly Papuan campaign freshly in mind, the Federal Ministry and its military advisers evidently know that if Australia can clear the Japanese out of the area provided in the bill now before Parliament, a good job will have been done, and the price of it will be most exacting to this thinly-populated nation. To that fact must be added this most important possibility: **Australia herself is still not free from the threat of invasion.** With our limited man-power we may be called upon at any time to resist enemy landings in our north or in the west.

Letters, T McEvoy. In the midst of their confusion of face loyal Australians must wonder how the niggardly provisions of that latest folly of war-time party politics, the Militia Bill, will be received in London, Washington, and Moscow. But what a laugh they will create in Tokyo, Berlin, and Rome. A nation fighting for dear life, virtually refusing assent to its military commanders for the unrestricted use of all its fighting men. And all for the sake of an academic adhesion to an outmoded political scruple.

Few of us, if any, doubt the sincerity of Mr Curtin in his desire to get on with the war, but the fact that he is bound hand and foot to a junta of trade union leaders is one of the many political pills we have had to swallow since his party came into power. It is evident that Mr Curtin's future as a member of his party, not to speak of his leadership, would have been jeopardized had he taken a strong and independent stand on questions such as coalition government and strikes.

His reputation, and that of his party, might conceivably have survived the shocks which the Australian public has sustained on these issues. It is difficult, however, to see how the country can overlook and forgive this latest outrage on its sense of national pride and international decency.

Letters, C R L L. We hear much loose talk as to how ashamed we should feel to think that America is sending her men and material to fight for the protection of our country. It must not be forgotten, however, that the use of this continent for the USA troops has given America a strategic benefit without which her offensive against Japan would have been made doubly difficult.

It is high time that we Australians took a more appreciative view of our own stupendous war effort and ceased to promulgate our own political and internal differences to an outside world which only too often sees them in a greatly exaggerated light and arrives at altogether false conclusions.

Letters, Veritas. We hope that there soon will be a peace conference – which the Allies will enter as victors. Mr Curtin will tell the world of what Australia considers her sphere of influence in the Pacific. That this limit has been defined simply as a matter of political expedience will not concern our allies.

It is not so many years ago that Australia protested to France against the sending of convicts to New Caledonia, and France agreed to stop doing so, but our politicians today are announcing to the world that New Caledonia is no concern of ours, nor yet the New Hebrides, the Solomons, and other strategic islands in the Pacific.

Our leaders portray Australia as a static nation, not a rising one. Absolutely without vision they consider great and grave questions, not from a national standpoint, but from a party aspect. We, by electing them, probably deserve the politicians we have, but how unfortunate for those to come!

OTHER MATTERS

Letters, DISGUSTED. Why are the Man-power authorities hunting up domestic servants, and as they term it, "women not gainfully employed", while numbers of young able-bodied girls and men are still conducting beauty parlours and women's hairdressing saloons? Surely, in a country at war with a ruthless enemy, the people could be in a war job, and if these luxury parlours must be kept going, their places filled by women over the call-up age.

Letters, Dorothy Ironmonger. There are few women in this country who will not wish the "Women to Canberra" movement well. However, one feels that it would be deplorable if the movement were to develop into a mere stampede for Parliament of ambitious women.

Surely, more important than whether representatives in Canberra are women or men is that the voters should take an enthusiastic and intelligent interest in politics. The ideal is that members of Parliament are placed there to do the will of the minds of the electors. Good government depends essentially on the electors having minds and wills. It was reported at the last meeting of the movement that "young people were not interested or were not seized with the seriousness of the matter." This seems to me to be the crux of the situation – that stimulation of the interest of the young and all women who are apathetic to politics should be one of the main objects of the "Women to Canberra" movement.

I would urge that the "Women to Canberra" movement undertake as one of its main objectives, some form of education and stimulation of women's interest in political affairs. Women representatives in Parliament would then come as a natural corollary, and not something forced by a few ambitious enthusiasts.

MARCH NEWS ITEMS

Five children died in Newcastle Hospital yesterday from burns received when explosive powder, which they had **extracted from a flare bomb**, was ignited. They were holidaying at Scarborough on Lake Macquarie, when they found the bomb.

A new War Loan of 100 million Pounds, to be known as the Third Liberty Loan, will be opened on March 16th. Australians will be asked to fill it in five weeks. The cash raised from such loans was being used for financing the War. Money loaned will be returned in the few years after the War. **Investing in the Loans was seen as being patriotic.**

March 6th. **London.** The Brits had been bombing Berlin for a full week, with massive resources. Tonight the Nazis sent off a retaliatory raid to London. It was a small, mainly unsuccessful excursion....

During the raid, people as usual **crammed into the tube underground stations**. In the rush to get into the shelter, a woman carrying a baby tripped at the bottom of a flight of stairs and **those following fell over her**. People could not advance or retreat, and new arrivals fell on top. **178 persons suffocated,** and another 60 were hospitalized.

The Man-power Department announced yesterday (Sunday) that **married women under 35 would be called up** in the Municipalities of Sydney, Coogee, Woollahra, Vaucluse and Bondi, to begin **work in canneries** on Thursday. These were very upper-crust suburbs.

Tuesday. Man-power said that the call-up of women had been deferred because of the **large number of women who had simply volunteered to work**.

Gandhi finished his fast on March 21st.

There was a multitude of complaints from the public brought about by **the presence of troops in Oz cities**. One example of this was the recurring riots in city hotels on Saturday afternoons where **huge numbers were involved**. The largest so far had seen 400 men in Melbourne brawling in the street. US troops were often involved.

Remember telephone operators? News item. Eight hundred girls are to be given permanent jobs in country telephone exchanges formerly staffed on a temporary basis.

The Real Estate Institute of NSW said that there is a shortage of 40,000 houses in the State. This was **the largest shortage ever**. The position was the same in all other States.

The Minister for Supply and Shipping said that by June 30th, Australians will have spent an average of **139 Pounds per head** on the War. The Basic Wage is 5 Pounds per week.

The Taxpayers' Association pointed out that under the **new pay-as-you-go tax legislation**, Australians would be paying **more tax per person than the British**. Also, they would not receive any post-war credits, as would the British.

Remember **Nestles' penny chocolates? Horse troughs?**

WAR NEWS

In March, the Russians met stronger resistance from the Nazi forces, and in a few places were forced to back-track. Still, mostly they were on top, and it still seemed that the War on the Eastern Front was going the way that the Allies wanted.

In the Pacific, the Japanese marshaled a fleet of 22 ships that started steaming south towards Australia. But it was badly mauled in the Battle of the Bismarck Sea, and the threat to Australia was accordingly reduced. Though MacArthur and Curtin, for their own reasons, continued to warn that the situation was still very threatening.

STRIKES IN WAR-TIME

Strikes continued to be a worry. The coal miners were **almost** top strikers of the month. But **quite outstanding** were textile workers, and most of these were women. They wanted 90 per cent of the wages of equivalent male workers, and they wanted decent conditions. There were all sorts of Government Boards and Commissions trying to settle these matters, but no clear picture was emerging. So these textile workers were taking matters into their own hands.

So, again, the papers were full of Letters, mostly condemning strike action. The arguments were generally that "our boys" were overseas fighting non-stop, under terrible conditions. Did **they** strike? Were the strikers aware that they were putting the lives of these "boys" at risk?

Many of these writers blamed the politicians. "Is there **no leader on either side of the House** with the courage to tell these strikers where they get off? Any such leader who advocated suppression of strikes would sweep the country, because it would allow Australians to hold up their heads and be as proud of their war effort and their Government as they are of their fighting men."

One writer made an interesting comparison. A Miss Harvey, of Marrackville, wrote that she worked in a factory where a strike was taking place. She compared her lot with that of servicemen, and found that the servicemen were better off than factory workers. "Out of her money, which is only 14 Shillings **more** than the serviceman gets, she must pay for her keep, clothes, fares. Perspiration and grease ruin clothes. Servicemen get their clothes free of cost. Shoes are very costly, and factory workers have to buy their own, as well as supply coupons.... Also, factory workers have no leave nor vacation with travelling passes to which to look forward to."

She added, that "Judging by appearances, sleeping on concrete floors (which servicemen supposedly do) plus their diet, is beneficial to their health, and not injurious, and at least they are working the fresh air."

As you might imagine, there were some vexed replies.

Letters, M Watson. Miss Harvey says the men in the fighting forces have free board and residence. Yes, often **the ground** to sleep on. Good meals? Tinned foods every day in the week! As for free new clothing, would it not often have been torn and sometimes covered in blood and mud?

It may be hot where Miss Harvey works; would the desert and the tropics be a littler warmer, and would there be seating accommodation there, and would they be able to have a shower and rest their weary bodies on a good soft clean bed at night? Would not "concrete" be better to stand on than being knee deep in mud with mosquitoes and the trying heat? Yes; they do get parcels occasionally, and just recently my husband received comforts from the Red Cross – he was in hospital. Does not Miss Harvey think that after a man has spent two or more years in the fighting front he deserves leave and free travelling passes? I do not think she really means what she says. If she thinks the men in the forces are better paid than she is she should join the forces herself.

Letters, Wm F Hunter, Secretary and Founder of the Textile Workers' Union, 1891. Although I have fought for the worker getting his just reward, it occurs to me that these strikes are a sort of mob hysteria, due to war; had the Federal Government taken a firm hand much earlier, many of these strikes would not have occurred. I regret Miss Harvey's drawing a comparison betwixt her own little troubles and those of the men who are giving their lives for their country. **It cannot be done.** I hope the girls will go back to work and help the boys who are giving their lives for them.

MEN'S CLOTHING AND MINISTER DEDMAN

Minister John Dedman was a very strong socialist, and thought the ideal State was one where the Government had control over most resources, both material and manpower. So when he came to Office, his dream had come true, and he could regulate and regulate to his heart's content. In my **1942 year-book**, I listed his extravagances in a number of places, so here I will simply remind you that it was he who introduced the famous ban on pink icing on cakes. Not white icing – that was OK. But if a shop sold cakes with pink icing, then everyone concerned in the purchase was liable to fines and imprisonment.

I must say that, to my knowledge, no one actually went to prison over pink icing. That was because people stopped using it. But **many** people **were imprisoned** because of breaches of his thousands of regulations. Let me give you an example. Mr Samual Ritenwax, trading as City Tailors, Sydney, had created a made-to-order suit for a customer to the correct specification of the Government, and the material was one of the three types allowed by the Government. But he had made it to actually fit the customer, and had charged 17 Pounds for it.

The regulation price for such suits, off-the-rack, was eight Pounds. For his efforts, he was charged with breaking the regulations, and **was sentenced to six months imprisonment**.

Letters, P Noster, Merriwa. The tailor who was jailed for making a suit that fitted did just that. He made a suit. If he had stolen a suit, he would have either been ignored by the police, or at the most, given a good-behavior bond by the Courts. But this George Street tailor did something far worse. He **made** a suit. This is a practice we must stamp out. Can you imaging what society will come to if we allow people to make things? **Much better we became a nation of stealers than a nation of creators.**

The tailor appealed against the sentence, and it went all the way to the **NSW State Supreme Court**. As a result, his conviction was quashed. I will not go into the devious reasoning that went on to get that result, but I will quote from the Court's decision.

Sir Frederick Jordan, speaking for the unanimous Court, said that he "**admired any trader who attempted to sell anything without having a lawyer and actuary at his elbow.** To try to arrive at the legal position it was necessary to thread one's way through a maze of intricate and obscurely-worded regulations. To judge from the many alterations that have already been made, the regulations appeared to be as stable as shifting sands.

"The framework and details of the regulations are wholly inept to cover the case of any person who manufactures any article to order, and **this prosecution is an attempt to use them for a purpose for which they are not designed.**"

At the same time as this rebuke was issued to Dedman and his Departmental colleagues, the man himself was forced to back-track on an earlier decision that had been met with widespread derision. He had defined an **Austerity suit** for men. This had no waistcoat, no cuffs on the pants, and was to be made from a very limited choice of materials. The number of pockets were limited, and fob pockets were out. Every suit made in Australia was supposed to conform to a few simple patterns.

His scheme struggled on for about a year, and then even he had to admit that it was a failure. Men-folk, and their wives, simply did not buy suits for that year. Manufacturers of material, and factories set up to produce them, were going broke. He finally stated that the regulations were to be amended to the point of extinction, and the entire population of the nation had one giant guffaw.

Mr Dedman, however, had a very thick hide. He went on undaunted, despite his intense unpopularity. He continued regulating all and sundry, and emerged from the war as by far the most pilloried Minister of the war years.

IS THERE NO OTHER NEWS?

The news from the war and the war effort took the headlines every day. There were restrictions of the amount of newsprint that the papers could use, and so the *SMH* could print only eight pages most week days, and perhaps 16 on a Saturday. Given that a few of these were taken up with classified ads, and a third of the remainder with feature ads, and one page with sport, there was a limit on the other material it could publish.

So if you picked up a week-day *SMH*, you could guarantee there would be **no non-military stories** on the first two pages. After that, local bits and pieces were spread across the next four pages, and then you were in the classified and sports news. Thus, less than 10 per cent of the news stories published were about non-military events.

But life outside war-time considerations did go on. Still, there were many attempts by politicians and **other fervid folk** to keep the war at the forefront of people's minds all the time. "Think about the suffering of our overseas sons. Remember how close the Japs got. Would you like to live with the same torturers as our prisoners-of-war have? No? Then keep working, produce more, work longer hours." Indeed, it was hard to get away from it all. At times, fortunately, most people managed to do that, and indeed at the moment their thoughts were straying further and further away from constant work.

There was one group though who were war-conscious **all the time.** These were **the loved ones and friends of the men who were doing the fighting.** For these people, there was little relief, and the fear every day of the dreaded letter from the Army was with them all the time. It was these people, generally, who were most vocal in urging others to greater patriotic efforts. It was understandable that they should be doing this. It was understandable too **for others** to be asking whether all of the effort being exerted was **now** needed, especially when the bureaucratic inefficiencies and wastage was so evident.

WOMEN TO THE RESCUE

The number of women who were serving their country was growing quite steadily. Some of them were in the Services, for example, as drivers and radio operators. Others were in factories, making textiles, munitions, tanks, planes, and bottling jam. Others were in the various forms of Land Armies working farms, and in the Civil Defence Corps making roads and aerodromes. There was another group who deserve mention. These were the host of women, living at home in the suburbs and towns, who quietly provided money and goods to keep our soldiers alive and well. These women raised money through raffles, fashion shows, morning teas, cake stalls, balls and dances, donations, and anything they could. Some of them were big society types, and many of them were poor and down-and-out. Lots were mothers of servicemen, and lots more were not. From all levels of society, these women steadily did what they could, non-stop.

They helped in other ways. They knitted socks, and balaclavas, and jumpers, they made camouflage nets, sent parcels of food and goodies all over the world. They staffed Red Cross and Comfort Funds and dozens of other groups.

These were unsung heroes, not risking their lives, but still ready to do anything they could to help.

When you put them all together, that's a lot of effort. When our fighting heroes are remembered, it would be proper to sometimes remember the massive forces supporting them at home.

OTHER MATTERS

I have included below some different material. A lot of it is a bit silly, but it gives some idea of what life in the suburbs and towns was all about.

Letters, North Shore. Recently my laundry lost one of my shirts, and in a letter admitting the loss, suggested that I call upon the Rationing Commission with a view to seeing what could be done about coupons when ordering another shirt to replace the lost one. I was informed that in addition to the laundry's letter, it would be necessary for me to lodge a statutory declaration setting forth every item of clothing in my possession. Could anything be more ridiculous? What possible relationship can the number of overcoats, boots, hats, etc., I possess, have to the missing shirt? It appears to be just another of the many absurd and annoying regulations that the public have to put up with, and it is high time that they were scrapped and replaced by something that has at least some suggestion of common sense at the back of it. What are we coming to?

Letters, No Honey. Is there a scarcity of man-power? Before the war honey was 7½d per lb (supply your own container). Now there is no "loose" honey, but it may be bought in 11oz jars for 10d and 24oz jars for 1/9½. These are new jars, new lids, new labels, and fresh adhesive. All this requires man-power and machines.

No allowance is made for empty returned honey jars; in fact, they are not wanted.

Letters, James MacFadyen, Clarence River. The price of fish is governed by the law of supply and demand to a greater extent than that of any other article, whatever its nature. If there is such a law – and who would deny it? – why not allow it to govern the trading in this article of diet, with a steadying on the rein of soaring prices of meat, rather than the revolutionary methods adopted? The reduction of fish prices is so severe as to be in some cases a reduction even on pre-war rates, and if some of the lower individual prices are taken into account, **the prices are such as to preclude the fish ever being seen in the market at all, as expenses would not pay the freight from these parts (Grafton) and many others.**

Letters, K Willoughby. The often expressed desirability of bringing into greater conformity to religious doctrine and modern education is given point in the **opposition expressed by the Christian Fighting Front to combating venereal disease** by the use of prophylactics and to the teaching of sex hygiene in the schools.

If these good people believe that this serious social menace can be eliminated simply by appeals to the moral or Christian conscience of the promiscuously inclined, they should bear in mind that the state of affairs today reflects the failure of the Churches to effect a remedy, notwithstanding nearly 2,000 years' effort by them along those lines.

One has only to contemplate the terrible suffering of many innocent children of infected parents, and to consider the danger to the virility of the race, to have more than sufficient reason to reject doubtful ethical scruples for a policy of greater realism.

Letters, Wm Murray. After giving full weight to the opinions of your correspondent, K Willoughby, the following considerations should not be overlooked. **Virtuous living is the only real remedy for the evil in question,** and the nostrums of science are merely patching up expedients. If Christian teachers during the last 2,000 years have not succeeded in making everyone virtuous, they have at all events achieved a limited success, for which they should be given credit. But for this limited success would the human race have survived, and would we be here to discuss this subject today?

Letters, Amicus. The civilian population is rationed in milk, and in many other things too numerous to mention. **The time for rationing beer is long overdue.** It is pitiful to see the number of young soldiers in the streets of Sydney who are the worse for liquor. Their mothers give their sons, if necessary, to die on the battlefield; but not to have them ruined by drink on the very threshold of their lives.

Letters, Richard White. I can sympathise with "North Shore." Last October I happened to be in Newcastle. I sent off a bundle of washing (30 pieces) to a laundry, the laundry was burnt out, and I lost everything. I made application to the Rationing Committee, and they asked me to declare how much stock I had at home. After declaring same, I was allowed coupons sufficient to purchase three pieces only by way of replacement.

Letters, L Turton. As I forecast some months ago, milk rationing has again been introduced in the City of Sydney. This will be more severe in the near future. The position has been forced on the milk consuming public by the very people who promised cheap milk to the consumer at electioneering time. Another factor which aggravates the shortage is the slow but sure strangulation of those engaged in the raw milk trade in the metropolitan area. If the Milk Board will not allow dairymen a price commensurate with their costs, who can blame dairymen for **changing over to pasteurised milk**?

Letters, Mother of Sons. Why should Anzac Day be kept as a holiday? Was it a holiday for the original Anzacs? Should it not rather be celebrated as a Holy-day, and remembered as such on the Sunday nearest to April 25? Then this farce of "keeping-it-up" on the Tuesday following would be unnecessary, and one day's waster of munitions and labour for the war would be averted. But in the welter of strikes and wastage, one day hardly counts to us, though it is a boon to the enemy. How they must jeer at our self-indulgence tactic! We could learn a few salutary lessons from them, but who wants salutary lessons?

Letters, Ex-Nurse. In view of MacArthur's recent warning, it seems incredible that Cabinet should consider granting at least four days holiday for Easter. Let us feel thankful that the fighting forces will not decide to go on leave, too, nor will they demand double pay, as civilian workers do when asked to help defend their country by working on any day that would be classed as a holiday in peace-time.

How much valuable time and money we could save if we made up our minds to forget all holidays, including week-ends, and worked on a roster system for the duration of the war. Hospitals and other institutions do this, so why not war industries? Five days on and one off, for instance, would enable workers to attend to private business on week days, and, perhaps, minimise absenteeism. It should also help to eliminate over-crowding of trains and other transport at week-ends, and need not prevent workers attending evening church service, as Sunday hours could be arranged accordingly.

Letters, (Rev) L M Thompson, Secretary, Baptist Social Questions Committee. We are amazed that Alderman Bartley should suggest the abolition of raceless Saturday. We feel that the great commercial enterprise called "racing," with its thousands of trainers, jockeys, stable attendants, bookmakers, clerks, and groundsmen, would be better employed in the conduct of the war if racing were abolished for the duration. The Premier of South Australia is the only Premier of any State in Australia with the courage to act upon this evident fact.

It is estimated that 83 million Pounds yearly is spent in upkeep, totalisators, and gambling to keep the Australian turf as an Australian sport. In a day of total war there is no justification for such waste of money and of man-power. Soldiers need arms before comforts, and if comforts are good munitions are better. There are thousands of women in our churches who spend hundred of hours knitting and sewing for the ACF; these do not desire an increase in racing with its attendant evils.

Letters, M W Burns. The suggestion that all letters for prisoners of war should be typewritten is hardly a practical one. As few people possess typewriters, the letters would first have to be written then sent away for the necessary typing, thus involving delay and waste of labour and stationery. Also, the letters would tend to become stiff and formal – not the sort of letters our boys want.

APRIL NEWS ITEMS

The movie "The Mummy's Tomb" was released in the Cessnock coalfields. It starred **Bud Abbott and Lou Costello**, and they were their usual sophisticated selves. A review in the *SMH* said it was **painfully bad**. However, at least one small boy, from Abermain, thought it was **the funniest movie that had ever been made.** He gave it five Stars.

Australia's 9th Division was now back home after Churchill had delayed them for up to a year. These were the troops who had done so much in North Africa in places such as Tobruk and El Alemein. **A crowd of half a million welcomed them as they paraded in Sydney** April 3rd. The Prime Minister, Mr Curtin, acknowledged that "we are all deeply thankful that, steadily and surely, the nation **has been coming safely through** one of the most tragic and devastating wars in history." Up till this date, Curtin had maintained that we were still under a real threat of invasion. Today's statement was **a welcome and reassuring change in tone.**

Military authorities in Britain and America said that **German submarines were more effective** than previously. They gave no details, but **the situation must be pretty bad** to have the spokesmen admit to such a situation.

April 14th. Sixty thousand Civil Defence workers, 4,000 Sydney wharf labourers, and 2,000 women munitions workers, **who had all been on strike, went back to work yesterday.**

April 20th. **Today is Hitler's 54th birthday.**

The use of public motor vehicles, like buses, for **pleasure tours in NSW** must be discontinued by order of the Commonwealth Land Transport Board.

Companies wishing to produce **bricks, roofing tiles**, fibrous plaster sheets, or crushed stones and the like, will be able to do so in future after they are **licensed by the Department of War Organisation.**

April 18th. In future, **organised sport**, open to the public, **will be banned on public holidays**. This applies to football matches, cricket, gymkhanas, horse-racing and the like. The reason given was that workers employed in essential industries were tempted to miss work and attend the sports.

April 21. The regulation banning sport on public holidays **has been amended**, and now applies only to events within **50 miles** of any **munitions establishment**. It was thought that persons outside that range would not be tempted.

The Minister for Trade and Customs said that **tobacco supplies to the public** would be increased from 50 per cent to 70 per cent of peace- time consumption per head.

Easter Sunday, it is generally said, falls on the first Sunday, after the first full moon, after the 21st of March. So we all get to March 21st , and say when is the next full moon, and work out the date of the next Sunday after that. But **this year it was tricky.** The definition should include a reference to **"full moon at Grenwich in England".**

Humbugs have gone from the store shelves. Oh dear.

A TOUGH LOOK AT EUROPE

The Russian war against Hitler had gone much quieter. On all points of the battle front, the Russians had won huge victories, and inflicted massive losses on the Germans. Mind you, in most places, **the Nazis were still occupying Russian soil**, but it was clear that Germany was in trouble. By the end of April, it seemed that both sides were getting ready for a Spring offensive soon, and that might well be a deciding point in the War.

Elsewhere, the Germans were under great strain in Tunisia, and in fact were soon to capitulate fully. The submarine war was going badly for Britain, and too much tonnage was being lost. This remained a sore point for Britain. They could and did send off large numbers of bombers each night to attack Nazi-held lands in Europe, but the German subs were still taking a terrible toll. Britain could not relax at all till the sub menace was brought under control.

A new theme was slowly appearing in the bulletins issued by Allied authorities. These included politicians, Army heavies, and the press. It was that, maybe, sometime, consideration would be given to a landing by the Allied forces somewhere in Europe, and land forces could set themselves for destination Berlin. It was all very vague, but it was clear that the Russians would like the opening of a Second Front. Would the rest of the Allies consider this? Was the time right? The answer to both questions was "maybe."

A SUMMING UP IN AUSTRALIA.

On April 13th, John Curtin released some valuable figures. I do not like quoting numbers, but in this case they really aid understanding.

Curtin said that the nation had 5 million persons of ages from 14 to 65, and these were split about equally between males and females. Of the 2.5 million males, 1.5 million were engaged in war occupations. This was about the same ratio as in Britain, and was nothing to be sneezed at.

These 1.5 million men could be divided into **three** categories. **Firstly,** there were the 800,000 men in **the Armed Services**. **Then** there were 500,000 in **factories**, including munitions. **The remainder** were in Government employ as **members of the CCC**, which I will explain in a minute. On top of that, **one million males were doing, or not doing, other things**. Again, I will return to these in a minute.

The bulk of the 800,000 men in the Armed Services were in the Army. The males were being paid six and a half shillings per day. That is, about 45 shillings per week. **The basic wage at the time was 100 shillings per week,** so you can see that the Diggers were not getting at all rich. Still, when that war was over, and they were de-mobbed, they would be handed a lump sum of deferred pay. On top of that, it could be argued, they got free food every day, free uniforms, and free accommodation. Some of this accommodation was in slit-trenches filled with mud and vermin in monsoon conditions, under enemy fire, in New Guinea, say, **but it was free, if they lived through it**.

After those, there were the men and women in factories and the CCC. The Civil Construction Corps was basically conscripted labour that had been called upon by Government to serve anywhere in Oz to do all sorts of semi-military tasks. Like building bridges, or air-ports, or roads. Or perhaps to work farms, or pick crops. The members of the Corps generally lived in camps like the military and had their own uniforms. They were not so regimented as the military, and better paid.

The factory workers were employed in munitions factories, and generally in manufacturing or pre-fabrication. They made goods that were classified as essential to the war effort. They were employed under various Industrial Awards, and were paid overtime and penalty rates. Given that many of them worked a fifty-or-more hour week, they **were better off financially than they had ever been**. By now, as a class, they were getting pretty tired of the long hours and the tough conditions. They had plenty of money just working 40 hours per week, and they were almost convinced that the great rush for more production was unnecessary. So absenteeism among their ranks was becoming a bigger problem.

When Curtin was eating his hotcross buns at Easter, he might have looked on the situation with some satisfaction. This level of organisation of a nation's population had been achieved from scratch in just 16 months. With all its faults, it was still a remarkable achievement, and it speaks well of the (wiser) men in charge and of the population that so much had been achieved. Overall, he could have been well satisfied with the position.

MANPOWER AUSTRALIA IN ACTION

As Curtin had pointed out, there were **a million males who were not involved in war occupations.** Many of these were exempted from such duties because of a variety of legitimate reasons. For example, some were medically unfit, some so bad that they were full-time cripples. Others had asthma, or TB, or polio. Or useless arms.

The largest number of exemptions were given to people in **Reserved Occupations**. These include coal-miners, wharfies, and dentists and doctors and lawyers and the like. Farmers, and some of their children were sometimes excluded, and certain employees of local Councils. Until recently, sales staff in Department and other stores were also not called up, but these people were now under close scrutiny. Small businesses were generally left with enough employees to keep going, but this was by no means certain.

The big authority for these one million people was Manpower. It had the authority to order any of these people to report to some location and to work as directed. So the destination could be the Army, or it could be with the CCC anywhere in Oz, or in a food factory on Mildura. These were extensive powers, and would have taxed any long-established governmental agency to the full.

This agency, though, was only a year since its conception, and had been stapled together with men who had no experience at all in this type of work, and they had none of the nation-wide vision that they needed. So, putting it briefly, the whole thing was a great wriggling mess. Half the conversations in the suburbs and towns, and half the Letters to the newspapers, were taken up with discussions of the anomalies and injustices stemming from Man-power's poor judgment and unfairness. Let me illustrate with a recent instance of abuse of power.

Over the last few weeks of April, Man-power, in its zeal, appeared to over-step its mark. It had raided three Sydney and one Melbourne nightclubs in peak business hours. It had even gone on to raid Sydney's famous Tattersall's Club in the same manner. It had sealed all entrances, and then processed the hundreds of patrons in each club, one by one. It demanded that everyone show their Identity Cards, and explain **how they had time to be in the clubs at that time**. It also wanted to know what work the person did, and whether they were exempt from **war occupations**. Those persons who failed to satisfy were required to report next day to the Man-power office for further interrogation.

Everyone was conscious of Man-power's requirements to recruit workers, but perhaps this was going too far.

News item. Mr Spender, MP, said yesterday that "the detention of people in public places was never intended when the Man-power regulations were passed. The power to detain people in a public place," he added, "is a different power from that requiring people to produce an identity card.

"If the man-power authorities have the power to detain citizens, it seems that they have equal authority to enter a man's home and detain for inquiry any of his friends. This is characteristic of the methods adopted by our enemies. This policy is being carried out under a Labour Government which mouthed about the liberty of the subject when in Opposition.

"No one disputes that the man-power authorities have the right to call upon people to produce their identity cards and to ascertain that they are properly engaged on work for the nation, but the methods of carrying out their work flagrantly and unnecessarily disregard the principles of Democracy. The man-power authorities have a difficult task, but it will not be made easier by antagonising the public."

In the face of public criticism, Man-power did not persist with this tactic for finding workers. It had, however, made its point with much publicity. It was on the prowl, and war-dodgers needed to be aware lest they got caught. Or, in effect, turn themselves in.

CURTIN'S LOAN APPEAL

With **a week to go**, the Commonwealth's Third Loan was **only half full**. Curtin addressed the nation in emotional tones.

"I said that we will be faced with a longer war than the war in Europe. That means that the attrition upon this country will be a prolonged attrition. That must mean certainly that our requirements in ships, in railway trains, in roads, in all the equipment that will go upon them will continue to increase. We cannot afford to dissipate anything now, because in **a year's time** we will be **still** fighting to hold this country, holding it, not only for our own sakes, but as a vital base which the United Nations will use for the purpose of completely destroying the enemy in the Pacific Ocean."

"I know that every gallon of petrol that is wasted in taking a car to a football match or a racecourse is a gallon of petrol that one day might stand between a bombing plane getting back to its base and not getting back to its base.

"Therefore I preach tonight against waste because I know that so much if it goes on. It goes on primarily because **the public prefers to spend its money in the shops rather than to give it as a direct contribution to the Government.**

"This Government or any other Government would not be worth its salt to the Australian people if it did not bring that fact plainly to the people; if it did not say to the people, **"Fill this loan, or else—.""**

There were some different ideas on this Loan.

Letters, Common Sense, Sydney. We are supposed to be at war for our very existence. Judging from the congestion on racecourses, in hotel lounges, dining-rooms, and bars, black marketing in petrol, liquor, and other commodities – it appears to be a "free for all" in a section of the community to gain as much as possible whilst the war continues.

A war cannot be fought without roads, aerodromes, etc. Why should the men who make them be paid several times more than the fighting men who use them and are ready to die in the attempt? **Cut the basic wage and awards** to **the level of soldiers' pay** and so make a practical effort to impose a more equitable sacrifice on all sections, and in turn reduce the initial war expenditure by many millions of pounds.

Letters, R Colman. While there is no gainsaying the fact that Australia must have the necessary money to finance our war effort and carry it to a successful conclusion, the limited subscriptions to the third Liberty Loan point to the fact that people are taking this means of telling Mr Curtin that they do not approve of the socialistic policy being enacted by Messrs Dedman and Ward under guise of National Security Regulations. If Mr Curtin will call in the best brains of all parties, and form a National Government, in which the people have confidence, I do not think he will have any difficulty in getting all the money he requires.   At the same time everything points to the fact that **compulsory loans** will have to form part of the financial policy.

Letters, Marion Leslie.   When I had recovered from the fit of weeping brought on by the spectacle of a dead soldier spread across a full page war-loan advertisement in the press – a soldier who could have been my dearly loved only brother who was killed in action – I was seized with a deep and red-hot indignation at its callousness.

At a time like this, when our country and liberty are in danger, we do not want "What will you do today?" yelled at us in one and a quarter inch type. We want the Government, which is in a position to know the extent of our danger and what is necessary to combat it, to tell us what to do and see that we do it without all this propaganda, which is an insult to our intelligence. Why cannot our leaders rise to the occasion and have the courage to admit that they made a mistake in opposing the raising of money by **compulsory loans**? With the exception of those who are using the war as a means to gain something for their miserable selves, **the vast majority of Australians would welcome this only fair way of sharing a burden.** It is up to our Government to show us our duty. Our soldiers did theirs when they gave their lives; do their dead bodies have to be dragged before our eyes before we will do ours?

Letters, Broad Shoulders.   I have been reading Mr Curtin's appeals for this Third Liberty Loan, and of the 2,000,000 people who don't see fit to lend their share of the vital money. I might say, before I complain of these "dillbrains," that my wife and I have been subscribing to every loan to help win this war. They say lend till it hurts; well, we are almost unconscious with pain from lending, but we are happy about it.

Too much money is held by these "dillbrains." Some of these, I can state, are mad with money, and dangerous to our country. I watched an auction sale last week, and I wish Mr Curtin could have been there. Let me quote some purchases by these "dopes."

Wireless set, value 52 Pounds, sold for 62 Pounds; cedar bed, value 6 Pounds, sold for 20 Pounds; a refrigerator, value 75 Pounds, sold for 150 Pounds. These are a few instances, but the best one was the price paid for scrap kitchenware – for on old pot, chipped and not very nice to look at, value nil, some fool thought fit to bid 10/- and almost had it, when another "dillbrain" shouts 12/6 and gets it, with a smile of victory.

Just think what the amount of loose money at this particular sale could have done for our boys over there fighting for us – money wasted, because **they had too much to spend.** Why?

Letters, Disheartened Aussie. We have the spectacle of the Prime Minister exhorting, with all the power of words at his command those who are earning such huge wages through the war, to put some of it into the third Liberty Loan – with such pitiful results. Those heartrending appeals touch to the quick patriotic people who have put all their effort into winning the war, but hundreds of thousands **getting incomes undreamed of before the war** would rather fritter it away on their own selfish pleasures, without a passing thought of the nation's pressing needs. And still the much needed Act of Parliament for **compulsory war saving** is not brought in.

Mr Curtin has given out two alternatives: "Lend all the money you can or suffer the dire consequences by a savage enemy." Why risk the latter when the Government could conscript the money and not injure those shirkers who will not shoulder their responsibilities as citizens of Australia? The money is in the country, and, as the Prime Minister truly says: "It will be a disgrace to our nation and most heartening to our enemies" if the loan fails.

MacArthur's WAR

Douglas MacArthur was keen to be seen as the great man who beat the Japanese, and knew from his earlier years that to do that meant he had to sell himself to the American public. So his headquarters in Brisbane sent out a constant stream of communications to the US telling them of his exploits and the victories, large and small, of the troops under his command.

Daily he would send a dozen cables telling wonderful tales of how he was beating the Japs to a pulp. But then he would send other cables saying he was in desperate need of more troops and equipment, and that the Japs were massing somewhere ready for a huge strike on the Allies. The two messages he was giving did not gel. Newspapers columnists in the US, not all of whom were fans of MacArthur, were asking sarcastically if there was some inversion of normal logic down in the South West Pacific so that the more victories we had, the worse our position seemed.

Incidentally, MacArthur's propaganda machine was working well within Australia as well. Lots of Press releases each day, and lots of newsreel clips. All such material suggested that the US forces were doing a great job, and occasionally Oz was seen to be helping out. Movie screenings in our capital theatres were constantly disturbed by catcalling and booing from Australian servicemen when they saw the glory these newsreels heaped on Americans and on America. A bit exaggerated, they thought, and a bit one-sided, too.

SHORTAGE OF RUBBER

News item. From April 21st, the speed limit for motor vehicles in all parts of Australia will be 30 miles per hour. (That is 48 kilometres per hour). Drivers caught exceeding this speed will no longer be charged under ordinary traffic laws, but under National Security Regulations. These carry stricter penalties, with the maximum fine set at 100 Pounds, with a maximum of six months imprisonment, or both.

The aim of the new regulations is to slow down traffic. This will conserve the rubber in **the tyres**, supplies of which are seriously short. Normal motorists must expect that no new tyres would be available for the duration of the War, and for many months after it.

OTHER MATTERS

Letters, Mary Edwards. May I plead with the authorities not to paint the bronze figures of the Cenotaph as has been done heretofore in preparation for Anzac Day? Penny chocolate soldiers and not allowed to gain the beautiful green patina of weathered bronze?

Letters, Woudn't It. On Saturday I counted 10 lusty young men in uniforms with trays of sweets lashed to their manly bosoms coming from a depot in Quay Street obviously bound for the jungles of some picture theatre in George Street South. Probably there are thousands of other youths similarly "gainfully" employed in other theatres.

Letters, H C G. "V J F," Bowral, may consider "Advance Australia Fair" an affliction, but it is infinitely more pleasant to listen to than many other national anthems. It speaks the spirit of Australia.

A NOTE ON LETTERS

Let me mention that most Letters would have been written by hand. That meant a pen with a nib, ink, ink pot, and blotter. They were written mainly at night under a 40-watt globe. So people who wrote them were serious and determined, and wanted their messages to be heard.

A NOTE ON MARBLES

This Letter describes the great tragedy unfolding.

Letter, Chips. The importation of marbles has stopped. First went the strong glass types with their wonderful colourful internal spirals and spectra. Then, even the china ones went off the market.

At the same time, local and then international competitions went.

Now, marbles as a game is dying out.

I warn you that as we stop playing sports like marbles, we as a nation will get fatter and look like Americans.

MAY NEWS ITEMS

In Europe, it was becoming obvious that **sabotage** against the Axis powers was becoming more common and the **guerilla forces** in places like Greece and Yugoslavia were becoming more active. This was partially because the Allies have now **found ways to get weapons to them**.

The Controller of Knitted Goods has been given authority to **issue permits** for the manufactures of **knitted cardigans, frocks**, blouses, slacks and skirts. Manufacture of these articles **was stopped** by an order issued last March.

New ration books will be issued to **six and a half million citizens** on June 5. No statement has yet been made as to how much of each commodity a coupon will allow. **Will the rations be cut?**

German resistance in Tunisia has been **totally defeated. All of North Africa in now in the hands of the Allies.** Talk of landings on the continent of Europe is coming from everywhere, especially from people who know nothing.

To help the Australia-wide campaign against **venereal disease**, the Federal Government has made a special grant of 25 million Pounds to the Commonwealth Health Department.

New ration books will be issued to **six and a half million citizens** on June 5. No statement has yet been made as to how much of each commodity a coupon will allow. **Will the rations be cut?**

May 15th. The Prime Minister said that the Government considered it appropriate for churches throughout Australia to **ring their bells** and hold thanksgiving services on Sunday in **recognition of the victory in Tunisia**....

The victory will allow the Allies almost **complete control pf the Mediterranean**, and this would speed up the flow of materials and weapons to the East. It would also allow air attacks to now be **diverted to European targets**.

May 17th. During a **"victory bells" session** on National Radio, **celebrating the win in North Africa**, the Prime Minister said that victory is definitely in sight. Calling for an all-out war effort, he added that "Our hearts have been lifted up, but there is much more to do. It shall be done – on the battlefield, in the workshops, in the mines, in the factories, and on the wharves."

In his address, he talked about **interrupting the production** of war materials as **"treachery"**. **This means strikes.** His mention of the wharfs and mines seems to indicate that those bodies of men might be in the firing line if he **ever** gets round to actually fighting strikes.

May 19th. The **Australian hospital ship**, Centaur, **was sunk** by an enemy submarine in the North Queensland area on a trip from Sydney to Port Moresby. A total of **299 people were killed,** and 64 survived. The dead included 18 doctors and 11 nurses. There were no patients on board. The ship sank in three minutes. The ship **complied with all the provisions of international law for hospital ships**, including being fully illuminated and marked with Red Crosses.

The defeat in Tunisia cost the Axis powers dearly. The present count of prisoners-of-war stood at 224,000, and large amounts of munitions and equipment were also captured.

The Director of Agriculture said that unless home gardeners grew **more vegetables** in their **home Victory Gardens**, domestic shortages would occur, with grave nutritional reactions, especially in children.

Venereal disease is a **major problem for the military**, and much man power is lost through it.

The Controller of Knitted Goods has been given authority to **issue permits** for the manufactures of **knitted cardigans, frocks**, blouses, slacks and skirts. Manufacture of these articles **was stopped** by an order issued last March.

General Thomas Blamey said that **3,000 Australian men had lost their lives** in New Guinea in the last nine months. Most of these were **militia, and aged 18 or 19. Babies, gallant babies.**

A Bill was passed in Parliament that gave the Aborigines Protection Board power to give **full citizenship rights** to **approved** aborigines. Whether the Board would exercise that power remained a moot point. What individuals would benefit, and how many?

MAN-POWER FLEXING ITS MUSCLES

Man-power was created with the task of putting people to work for the war-effort by somehow rounding up anyone who was idle or not fully productive, and moving them to more useful tasks. The Director, and his deputy, were given the power by statute to direct any civilian living in Australia to engage in **any specified employment or perform any specified services.** This was a legitimate goal in war-time, and could well have been nation-saving. But in May, there were some **worries** that, useful or not, a monster had been created, and **individual freedoms were being sacrificed beyond the point that people would bear.**

In April it had raided night-clubs and impersonated the Gestapo. It copped a lot of flack from that. Then it harassed two Union Secretaries for placing stop-work ads in papers, in their normal manner. It got more flack. Incidentally, a week later, when this latter matter came to court, the action was dismissed because the Government did not want to proceed. Cooler heads had prevailed.

Now in May, it was not at all daunted by these two well-publicised foul-ups. It went out like the American FBI agent Elliot Ness, and raided all sorts of places. It invaded the premises of **the entire Sydney Kings Cross area**, and inspected every building for "draft-dodgers" or people not properly allocated to work. These were Sydney's truly sleazy suburbs, and their haul was a heavy one, and numbered about 500 men, mainly for the CCC. Anyone who had no identity card or was a slacker of any kind found themselves in the army or the CCC **within a week**.

News item. " Charged with having **failed to attend for medical examination** on March 16 when ordered to do so by the military authorities, Paul Shirley, 24, of Bourke Street, East Sydney was sentenced to six months' imprisonment by Mr Wells, SM, at Paddington Court yesterday."

A few days later they invaded racetracks in places as far apart as Maitland in NSW and Ascot in Victoria. Here they wheeled in, with local police, in cars that blocked the exits, and mustered everyone, and put them through the interrogation. It was all very dramatic, and once again got the publicity it sought. Ascot netted 100 men, again mainly for the CCC.

It was not just the fringe dwellers of Kings Cross and the touts at night-clubs and the race tracks that got attention. Fifteen hundred household servants were called in for questioning to see if any could be released for hospital duties. When householders complained about losing their home-help, the Director of Man-power advised them to "**do your own washing.**" Likewise, when he called up green-keepers from golf clubs, he had fired off a quick response to complaints. "**Mow your own greens. And use all your spare space to grow vegetables**."

All taxi-drivers in the Newcastle and Wollongong areas were given the treatment. Able-bodied shop girls could be found more productive work. The number of Council employees in many areas was halved. **The number of able-bodied persons working for Man-power was not disclosed**, though many people suggested that it might have increased somewhat.

The *SMH* Editorial sums up the response of the community.

The swoop of carloads of man-power officials upon Ascot Racecourse as the barrier was about to rise was in the best Hollywood tradition. It is a pity that the officials, owing to war-time restrictions to which even they must submit, could not each be equipped with **a cigar protruding at an aggressive angle from the corner of the mouth, as a recognised symbol of "toughness"** to overawe the cowering throng. The results of these excursions, in the form of extra man-power for essential work, are negligible, it is true, and, unless the organsiation is woefully weak, Mr Bellemore and his cohorts would surely achieve far more by a careful sifting of their own voluminous records than by sporadic and spectacular raids. But how much simple pleasure the man-power officers would miss were they to follow their own precepts and stick to their office desks, instead of exploring racecourses, restaurants, and hotel lounges! With what pleasurable thrills they must invade the precincts of a nightclub, even though their lack of sophistication leads them to stage the exploit in mid-afternoon, with the capture of but one elderly woman caretaker as reward!

News item. There would be further man-power "visits" and identity cards should be carried at all times, the Deputy Director-General of Man-power, Mr Bellemore, said yesterday.

"Notwithstanding criticism," said Mr Bellemore, "these visits are going to be continued. If people are found without their identity cards, they will be subjected to some slight inconvenience.

"The main purpose of the next visits we shall make will be to check holders of identity cards. For that reason the public are asked to carry their cards."

Letters, War Worker's Wife, Balmain. Since Christmas four hawkers, apparently able-bodied men, have called at my home. Why are not these men directed into essential work?

Letters, H Blake. The retail trade has been the object of much Ministerial derision. One could be led to believe, from the public utterances and threats of some Ministers that the retail store had no real place in the scheme of things, and was one of the scourges of modern life. Yet the retail trade, directly and indirectly, pays the bulk of the nation's taxes, and again, directly or indirectly, provides most of the nation's employment. Even a Governmental theorist should be able to see its economic place in normal times. Apart from those directly engaged in the retail trade, vast numbers of others employed in manufacture, in transport, and so on are dependent upon it.

Yet today the retail store is being willfully handicapped at every turn. Irritating and countless regulations, many of them without any apparent purpose are thrust upon it; taxes have mounted to alarming heights, and the biggest problem of every store at the moment is how to hang on and continue to function.

Letters, M Boole. The problem of a shortage of man-power is partly a shortage of Australian brain-power in using the available man-power.

TRADE UNIONS' WINNING WAYS

Trade Unions were getting braver and braver. They were almost thumbing their noses at Government, and daring it to attack them. But they were pretty secure because the Labour Government had only a majority of two in the Senate, and these two were Independents. Given that the voting base of Labour came from the Unions, the Government was not game to frustrate them. So the familiar battles went on.

To illustrate a little of this, I offer the four connected Letters below. They provide a good example of some of the disputations that went on in the work-place.

Letters, J. I am an employee of an aircraft factory, to which the boys in the battle area send their worn and damaged bomber engines for overhaul and repair. There are many of these damaged engines at the works, Australian and American, some with bullet-holes through and through them, awaiting attention.

Recently the workmen at the factory went on strike, because one of their union delegates was called up for the Army – of course he is sacred. Of the many hundreds of men and women employed in the overhaul section, five men, mainly fathers of the boys flying the bombers, decided to stand by the boys at the front and **continued to work**.

After having the union official exempted from the Army, the workmen returned to work with him; but immediately after getting things moving, threatened another strike if **those five loyal workmen were not sacrificed on the altar of unionism. They got the axe.**

Letters, Quandong, West Ryde. The story told by "J" is extraordinary. Did the facts stated really occur in Australia, for whose freedom heroes are dying? Several important points are raised by the letter: by whose authority were those loyalists in the factory (where damaged bombers are repaired) dismissed? Is it not true that no employee can be dismissed except for serious misconduct?

Letters, Loyalist. "Quandong" doubts whether the facts stated by "J" could be possible in this country. As I happen to be one of those who got the "axe" I should know the facts. In the recent strike at the aircraft factory over the call-up of a union shop steward, there were about 15 who refused to be embroiled in such a trivial matter but only about six were discovered. At the mass meeting at the Trades Hall, where the vote was taken on a call of voices in a packed hall, the result was very doubtful. On a show of hands it was beyond doubt that the majority wanted to return to work but the chairman refused to pass the vote and ruled it out as defeated. This action was disgusting in a meeting of men supposedly fighting for their freedom. One man who stood up to protest against the ruling was approached by two of the union representatives and threatened he would be knocked down if he did not shut his mouth.

This is the first fact of how the men came to go out on strike, and it needs no comment for any decent Australian to sum up the war efforts of the so-called unionists.

On returning to work after the strike, some of us were put through the third degree for remaining loyal to our job. We were given 24 hours to join the union and undertake to obey its rules and regulations, or else ask the management for a clearance.

We were told by the union stewards that we must be in the Union by 3 o'clock that day or they would stop work. We were called before the management for interview, and the hopelessness of the position was put before us. It was either the six of us ask for a clearance, or else 2,200 men went out on strike again. In other words, it was a technical dismissal. These are the facts leading up to the termination of our services at the factory, and

I trust they will open the eyes of all Australians to what goes on behind the scenes.

Letters, Frank Thompson, Secretary, Combined Unions Shop Committee. Regarding the letters by "J", "Quandong", and "Loyalist", on a recent dispute at a Sydney aircraft factory, almost every man and woman who ceased work had some close relative in one or other of the Services. Also there were many involved in the stoppage who were returned soldiers from the present fight against Fascism. Do your correspondents question the loyalty of these people?

"Loyalist's" remarks regarding the mass meeting in the Trades Hall are quite contrary to fact. He admits he was working during the strike, so how does he know what took place at the Trades Hall? The true facts of the decision of the mass meeting are that the resolution was moved, discussed at length, and carried in a most democratic fashion. When the chairman asked for "those against" not one vote was recorded. No one was threated or told to "shut his mouth." The best proof of the justification of the stoppage was the fact that less than a dozen workers in 2,200 disagreed with the decision to continue the stoppage, and the majority of this dozen proved to be anti-unionists.

It is traditional of Australian workers that they refuse to work with people who will not join their unions and who continue to work during a strike. "J" and his "loyal" mates are no exception to this rule. The war effort is too important to be held up by this un-Australian type of loyalty of such individuals. They are of no value to their own class, let alone our war effort, and will be the source of trouble wherever they work.

Comment. There were plenty of similar reports from workers, and plenty of denials from Union officials. Who is telling the truth?

PROBLEMS WITH FEEDING THE NATION

It was becoming apparent that various Government policies were substantially robbing the nation of its power to provide enough food for its civilian population.

One such policy was that priority in food distribution be given to the armed forces. **Every food that you can think of** was somehow bulked up and sent off to the military. This applied to the men overseas and to the majority who were stationed somewhere in Oz. In the latter case, reports of food wastage were many, and much civilian blood boiled when they became known.

Letters, A Mother, Balgowlah. For the past two months I have been unable to buy prunes for my two-year-old child. My husband is at present training with the RAAF in Sydney, and at least once a week the trainees receive a large helping of prunes as a dessert, most of which find their way to the pig tin, as they are unpopular with a large section of the men. Surely this is unnecessary. I can understand men in tropical climates and under battle conditions requiring this item in their diet but why a healthy group of men living in the city should be fed upon them whilst the babies go without I cannot understand.

The boiling of blood got more serious when it became obvious to all that **American troops were being fed much better than their Australian counterparts**. This was part of a deal that Oz had done, to guarantee the Yanks food of a certain quality.

Another factor was the depletion of production by the flow of men into the army and, later, the CCC. Farms were reporting that this year, crops could not be sown because sons and men-folk were absent and there was no pool of casual labour to hire.

Letters, Rachel Roxburgh. There has been great lack of foresight in draining our primary industries of skilled men who have been called from essential work to join the fighting forces. The source of our national wealth is thus being allowed to deteriorate shockingly. Everywhere in the country the story is the same: We usually have 1,500 acres under crops, but of course this year there's no labour and my husband is in camp.

One point appears to have gone unnoticed by the Man-power authorities. In factory and the fighting forces all work is supervised. New recruits are carefully trained to do what is required of them. But what chance has the solitary farmer or station holder to train the labour he occasionally procures. He is over-worked and only long experience can teach them. Any experienced countryman who leaves his job is practically irreplaceable.

Yet it goes on. Valuable dairy herds sold off for meat, sheep dying for want of attention, good land uncultivated, fences collapsing, and rabbits increasing furiously. It is not surprising that food is scarce. Young men naturally are anxious to join the forces when old enough. But the older and experienced men should stay and fight where they are, on the food front. As in Russia, why cannot key countrymen be kept at their tasks and do part-time Army training? After the war

Europe will need all the food we can send her. And we shall need the payment.

Then there was **price fixing**. The Government was anxious to stifle discontent over rising prices. Wages in factories and overtime payments meant that much of the population was better off than it had ever been. Inflation thus became a danger. So, the Government said that many prices, including those food-stuffs, were fixed at low levels. It turned out that these levels were too low to consistently support many farmers, who were inclined to stop or reduce planting and trading. Dairy farmers were particularly hard hit in this case. Day after day there were pathetic calls from mothers for more milk.

There were other restraints on production. For example, households in most States were allowed to keep about 20 hens in their backyard for egg production. Now, however, in view of the shortage of eggs supplies, there were calls to increase the limit to 40 hens. But these calls fell on deaf ears, so the population explosion was not forthcoming.

Comment. The Government was slowly waking up to the fact that people at home had to be fed, and that resources had to be deliberately allocated to food production. Curtin et al had been talking about this all through May, and at the very end of the month announced that a new position of Commonwealth Food Controller had been created. He also said that a similar position had been created in Papua to handle rubber and copra. The mooted plans for these controllers were very grandiose, and would create another huge bureaucracy. But for the moment, there was a long way to go, and it would take some time to assess their worth.

Letters, A Soldier's Wife, Burwood. On a recent public holiday the girls at our factory attended work as usual, and turned out an excellent day's production, regardless of the fact that many of them were late for work owing to the crowd of holiday-makers who thronged every vehicle of transport. When our day's work was done we encountered the same trouble, only more so, and some of the unfortunate girls waited over an hour on railway stations before they could even board a train. On the previous Saturday morning, also a public holiday, and the only day in the week on which we are able to visit the shops, we found all retail stores closed, while other able-bodied girls of our own age were away enjoying themselves. Many of the workers have homes to look after, and this naturally encouraged a morning's absenteeism during the next week.

The point I wish to stress is this. We, the workers, are the subject of heated debate in the clubs of businessmen, in the homes of housewives at their tea parties, and over the staff lunch tables in offices and shops. It appears that we "earn too much money" and too often "speak out of turn." Do those same ranting people ever stop to ask themselves why we earn that money, and what we have to do to earn it? We commence work at 8 a.m., and with only 30 minutes for lunch, we work until 5.15 p.m. Three days per week we work until 8.45 p.m. During this time we sit in a cramped position working at full pressure, and never ever see a ray of sunlight. We volunteered for this work during the first year of the war; we were not called-up and forced into it, and we are proud of the job we are doing for our menfolk in the forces.

But, of the general public, how many can say that they, too, are engaged in whole-hearted war effort? How many of you housewives spend your spare time in a canteen or the rooms of a comforts fund? How many of you business men are lending money to the war loan, not as a business investment, but interest free? And how many of those shop and office girls who regard us as beneath their social level responded to the appeals made to them by man-power officials to do an essential job? (In one suburb alone 147 out of 600!) During the recent public holidays who thronged the racecourses and picture theatres to squander money? Certainly not munition workers, who were at their posts as usual.

Let it be a case of "everybody in," with no distinction, and then, and only will we have reason to believe we can win this war to end all wars.

WAITING FOR AN INVASION

At the end of May, what a turn-round in Europe. Two months ago, all the Allies were uptight, fighting desperately on two fronts. **In the east**, the Russians were grinding ahead day by day, and expecting that the Germans would launch a massive summer offensive. But, at the end of June, things had gone quiet, and there was clearly no offensive on the way.

In Africa, the fighting in Tunisia was obviously going towards victory, but who would ever know what the Germans could pull off. Now, it was all over, the north of Africa had been cleaned up, and could be used to bomb and bomb any part of the Med and Italy. This is what had happened all through of June. The first question being asked everywhere was when would the Allies invade some part of Europe, and open up a Second Front?

The answer obviously was "soon". The next question was "where". Norway was often mentioned, but Italy was the outright favourite. Right now, it was having tons of bombs dropped on it nightly, in every one of its major cities, and especially in the south. Some of its small island possessions had already surrendered to the Allies. So that nation in particular was adjusting to the fact that the war was now on the other foot, so to speak. From being an aggressor nation, attacking other lands, it was now waiting for an invasion itself. **What a turn-round.**

Letters, Wallace Pooley. In England, the Amalgamated Engineering Union pledged itself to raise 150 thousand Pounds to provide Stalingrad with a new telephone exchange, the Association of Scientific Workers sponsored a special fund to equip a pathological laboratory in Stalingrad to be "the finest in the world." More notable still is the gift by the King, a Sword of Honour.

May I suggest that the City of Sydney should present a sum sufficient to build and furnish a **complete children's ward in the new Stalingrad General Hospital**, and that a plaque suitably inscribed (in Russian, of course) should be prepared here to be reset in the wall of the ward.

Letters, H Ward. We should look after our own pensioners and latch-key children first. To hell with the Reds.

JUNE NEWS ITEMS

June 1st. Man-power Officials today raided the Newcastle Express train soon after it left Hornsby on its journey to Newcastle. They questioned 217 men in order to check up on absenteeism and draft dodging.

The war in Europe was going well, including some improvement in the sub war. But keep in mind that during the last week, 121 Allied planes were lost in its four attacks on the Ruhr Valley. Worth thinking about.

A prominent Opposition Member, Mr Spooner, captured the mood of the nation when he broadcast that the current Government was a "Ministry of hush-hush socialists."

The Full High Court yesterday decided that the National Security Regulations, prohibiting publication of advertisements to promote the sale of Christmas, New Year and Easter gifts, were valid. Think about that too.

Australian casualties of the war from 1940 to March 1943 were the 10,200 killed, 21,900 missing, 24,300 wounded and 10,700 prisoners of war.

Wednesday, June 2nd. A notice gazetted on Monday authorising military police and Man-power offices to demand production of identity cards by civilians was cancelled yesterday (Tuesday) by order of the Minister for Labour, Mr Ward.

Australia was not the only nation plagued by strikes. In the US half a million mine-workers were now in their second day of strike.

Organised gangs operating near a number of Army camps are selling forged civilian identity cards and positions in protected undertakings to men anxious to desert. The question raised was that if the newspapers could find the sellers, why could not military police and Man-power?

June 5th. **New ration books for clothing, tea and sugar** will be issued today and tomorrow. British subjects (includes Australians) must present an identity card, a completed CR7 form, and their old ration books.

Butter will be rationed from June 6th. Each person will be allocated **half a pound a week.**

More than **3,000 German and Italian prisoners-of-war** are employed in useful work in Oz, the Army announced.

Under a newly gazetted order, **disposal or acquisition of new motor vehicles without a permit is prohibited.** Permits will be issued by the Director-General of Land Transport.

The Director of Rationing announced that it was **now illegal** for any school **to require pupils to wear a school uniform.** This order applied to all parts of the uniform, including stockings, hats and gloves.

In Europe, 2,000 tons of bombs were dropped on Dusseldorf, continuing **the daily bombing on German cities.** An indication of the record number of bombers used is given by the fact **that 43 aircraft are missing. Lest We Forget.**

One man died and two other persons were affected by carbon monoxide fumes while they were in vehicles fitted with **producer gas units** at the week-end. Remember those devices fitted to the rear of cars, or as gas bags on top?

UNITY IS STRENGTH

The Trade Unions were pushing their luck. In NSW, they had just seen legislation passed that said that preference in employment had to be given to unionists. This meant that if two persons with exactly equal qualifications applied for the same job, then it would go to the union member rather than someone who was not a member. Some other States were talking about similar legislation.

By **some extraordinary convolutions**, what this came down to in practice was that in industrial sites with militant unions, unionists were now refusing to work **if non-unionists were also employed on the site.** The justification for this was that it was costly to the Union to maintain wages and conditions, and everyone got benefits out of this. Therefore everyone should pay the union fees. And anyway, the unions needed grassroots support in their negotiations, and they could appear to have this only if **all** workers stood behind them. So pay your fees, do what we say, and stop talking about democracy and individual freedoms, you silly sheep.

I have said a lot about unions over the last few pages, and I won't wax too much now. Still, one particular situation that unfolded over the months must be reported. There was a factory, at a censored location near Sydney, that employed a thousand workers, men and women. About fifty of the women refused to join a union, and so the rest of the work-force walked off the job. The women said they would join a union if the union agreed in writing to three conditions.

These were that **firstly**, awards and decision of the (Federal) Arbitration Court would be obeyed where those awards were against the union as well as when they were in favour. **Secondly**, that strikes and stoppages (under Federal legislation) would not occur in that union for the duration of the war. **Thirdly**, that a secret ballot would be taken on the job on all major union matters.

These demands were quite logical and sensible – if you looked at Commonwealth legislation. **Strikes were forbidden, it was just that no one was enforcing that law at the time.** Most other people agreed that secret ballots would be a good thing, though union leaders knew full well that they would destroy their ability to manipulate the workers. Likewise the desire to stick by **all** rulings, either for your cause or against it, seemed to be a fundamental aspect of democracy.

So, the women got great Press coverage, and lots of public support, particularly from women. The question that was often asked was why would men not take a similar tack. Thomas Grahame of Elrington Colliery had a good answer.

Letters. If I vote against the union, my name is recorded for later revenge, and perhaps I am physically threatened. But worst of all, **I am branded as a scab**, and that not only blackens me but **my family for life**. No man would risk that, but no one would dare to do that to women because of public pressure.

As the strike dragged on, all Hell broke loose. Officials of all colours had their say and many invaded the factory itself to plead, argue, threaten, cajole, bargain or explain. Union leaders, Man-power, Court officials, Ministers of Government, the Women's Employment Board, all came and went in quick succession.

The leader of the women, a Mrs Cassidy, wife of a prominent K C, was a good-enough agitator and held the ground for them. She argued that they presented for work every day ready to go, but were told by management that the unionists were not prepared to work, and that they should go home. If anyone was breaking any law, it was the strikers.

Man-power was represented by a visit to the factory in person by its Director. He made a lasting impression by threatening the women, at the end of a frustrating session with them, that he could find plenty of work for them in the fruit canneries in the Riverina. Another gentleman, Jock Garden, as a liaison officer for the Minister for Labour, ended up assuring Mrs Cassidy that he would be happy to "bury her to the neck in dirt." Mr Garden claimed he had said "in work" not "in dirt" but there was still the feeling he was not happy.

Comment. We will come back to this dispute soon. In the meantime, note that the Federal Government time and again had threatened a tough line on strikes. The above episode illustrates the fact that the laws relating to unions were a mess, and that official attempts to stop strikes and control unions were farcical.

But, put simply, no prosecutions or punishments for striking were likely while the Government had such a slim hold on Parliament, and while a Federal election was due in a few months. Union support was vital to it survival.

BUTTER RATIONING

When butter rationing was introduced, everyone took the opportunity to grumble and grizzle a lot, though most people really accepted their lot without much ado. But not the miners at Hebburn Number 2 in the Cessnock coalfields. This pit was thrown idle next day as a protest against the severity of the rationing. Half a pound a week was not sufficient for a miner.

"After making provision for cut lunches, which he must carry to his work, a miner will have no butter for household work. The miners need the vitamins in butter. The mainstay of their crib is sandwiches. They have no canteen to augment their lunches. At least a double ration should be given every man working in a mine." These words from the Miners' Federation Secretary, George Grant.

Not everyone agreed.

Letters, L Westropp-Carey. Having travelled in many countries, including South America, might I say that I strongly approve of the butter rationing here? It should have been introduced much earlier so as to have built up supplies which could have been sent to Britain. Why did the Government wait till man-power shortage, together with the drought, made rationing compulsory? Half a pound per person is ample, especially compared with 2oz in Britain.

Letters, Dorothy Wrigh. I was both amazed and indignant to hear so many selfish protests against the butter rationing. In this country where, until this late date in the war, we have never been called upon to suffer any severe hardships or discomforts, surely we can willingly make such a minor sacrifice as this to help our mother country maintain her very meager supply of 2oz butter weekly.

England showed the whole world that while her very heart was being mercilessly bombed "she could take it." Let Australians rally round and show England that, small though our sacrifice be to aid her, "we can take it," too.

Letters, M J Dillon. I oppose the contention that the butter ration is too severe – eight ounces a week for every individual including babies, and the reason for the small sacrifice demanded of us is to maintain the ration in Great Britain at two ounces! The ration should be reduced to six ounces, or better still five ounces, thus making the share with Britain fifty-fifty. We are dealing with our own kith and kin, and what they have to take, we surely should be able and willing to take.

Unlimited local consumption of butter is expensive living and wasteful. There is nothing wrong with **good, clarified dripping** for children or adults. Here's hoping that the government will **not** allow itself to be dragooned into increasing the ration by senseless clamour, but will instead reduce it to five ounces.

Letters, Disappointed. Australia has missed a great opportunity. If the butter ration, at all events for adults, had been made 4oz a week, a good deal more would have been provided for Britain. The Old Country has managed for a long time on 2oz, the United States is making do with 3oz (in some States), whilst we spoilt children of fortune must have 8oz. Let the youngsters have their ½lb by all means, but surely 4oz is enough for any adult, and I am sure we would have obtained the respect of our kinsmen at home and our Allies, too, if this tiny sacrifice had been made.

Letters, One of the Others. Who are we in Australia that we should have more butter, milk, etc., than the other fighting nations? And later must all the burden fall on others to feed the people released from German domination? Give the "squealers" their extra coupons, marking them "Squealer coupons," and let the rest tighten their belts.

Comment. These were the only five butter-Letters published by the *SMH*. Apart from their unanimous support for butter rationing, notice they all reflect a thought that was prevalent in Oz at the time. That is, that England and Britain were to be given all the support we could muster. The ties of the British Empire were there for all to observe, and it was just a matter of course that we, every one of us, were bound to make sacrifices for the sake of the Old Country.

CURTIN CHANGES HIS TUNE

Half way through the month, Curtin did something quite remarkable. He went to talk Douglas MacArthur. The next day, he announced to a surprised nation that there **was now no threat of invasion**. Only a couple of weeks ago he was banging on about how serious the threat was, and that everyone had to accordingly keep their nose to the grindstone. Now he came out with the statement that the threat was there no longer. No beating about the bush, it had suddenly gone.

Of course, almost everyone already knew this, and it came as no bombshell to anyone. But the change in attitude in such a small time-frame did cause tongues to wag. Then he started talking to the unions, telling them how essential it was that they cut their strikes, because this was an election year, and voters would punish a Labour Government if the unions got too willful. His tough talk was disappearing, and he was simply telling them some home truths. Again, a big sudden change.

Something was going on in Curtin's mind.

SOMETHING TO CHEW OVER

I know you have all been waiting for my few pages on suet pudding. I know there are hundreds of readers among you who will be enthralled to enjoy the expertise of the following Writers, and I offer their tracts to you with enthusiasm.

Letters, Winifred Earl. Now that butter is rationed and there is a seasonal shortage of milk, eggs, and potatoes, perhaps a reminder of the virtues of the boiled suet pudding may be useful. Fats are our warmth-giving foods. In England a boiled suet pudding appears once or twice weekly in most households and large families. On inquiring among my friends here I find that most of us use suet (if at all) only once a year, for the traditional Christmas pudding recipe. A beef steak pudding needs to accompanying potatoes, while many varieties of sweet puddings made with apple, rhubarb, currants, or golden syrup need neither eggs nor milk.

Letters, F Thomason. Your correspondent who advocates suet puddings may have lost sight of the chief drawback to this class of fare with the low wage-earner, and that is the cost of gas. Boiled and steamed puddings take from two hours upwards to cook, and a kettle must also be kept boiling to "feed" the pudding as the water evaporates. Most low-rented houses have slot meters, and the cost of gas per slot meter is about double that of gas paid by a quarterly bill, notwithstanding the former is paid in advance. In England, the fire is going practically all the year round, and so soups and puddings which take long cooking are cooked at no extra cost.

Letters, Marguerite Gibson. Apropos your suet pudding advocate, may I say I, too, favour that humble pudding as a warmth-giving food.

Suet has the merit of being both wholesome and inexpensive. Perhaps the following recipe for the use of suet in a savoury pudding to serve with roast meats might be of use to readers: - ½lb of breadcrumbs. Pour over as much water as they will absorb. Cover and soak till soft. Beat with wooden spoon until soft. Boil three big onions, chop very fine, add to crumbs. Add ¼lb of grated suet, 1 teaspoon powdered sage, two tablespoons rolled oats, salt to taste. An egg may be added if desired. Mix all together, and bake in scone tray for 1¼ hours. Cut into slices and serve with roast meats.

Comment. In case there are a few readers who do not remember much about **suet**, I have a reference from a dictionary. It says that suet is the hard, fatty tissue about the loins or kidney of a cattle or sheep, it is used in cookery, and prepared as tallow. **Suet pudding** is a pudding mixture with suet added in place of butter and served with a sweet sauce.

MIND YOUR LANGUAGE

A Methodist clergyman complained from the pulpit about the use of the word "bloody" in an Australian film. This correspondence of two Letters speaks for itself.

Letters, Wesleyan, RAAF. Surely the height of narrow-minded intolerance was reached by the Rev F Rayward in his censorship of the Australian film "South-West Pacific" before screening at the Methodist owned and controlled Lyceum Theatre. The adjective he objects to is a perfectly good English word, as old as the language, and oft quoted by that master of our tongue William Shakespeare. Nowadays it is used to lend such force to an expression as no other word can. It may be crude, but it is neither obscene nor vulgar – the two evils from which Mr Rayward is quite rightly obliged to protect Lyceum audiences.

The word was used with telling effect in such excellent British productions as "Pygmalion" and "Journey's End," and in the Hollywood presentation of Priestley's "Good Companions." Surely all of these films could have been screened at the Lyceum without Methodism gaining any ill fame or Mr Rayward receiving criticism from the most pure in the land.

As in "Journey's End" and the Australian film "Forty Thousand Horsemen," the word was used because it was essential to realism. To delete it would have been as foolish as to strip the badges from the players' uniforms, wipe the blood and grime from their faces or the dirt from their boots. If the word is ugly and falls crudely on sensitive ears, it is merely in keeping with the subject of the film. War is crude and ugly, and in the sacred cause of peace should always be presented as such. Those who are in the fight would not want to have it glorified as in Axis countries.

As a Methodist and the product of a good Methodist home, I feel that Mr Rayward in his act of censorship renders a disservice to the cause of the Church, and gives its critics an example of wowserism which is unfair to thousands of adherents throughout the State.

Letters, W Smith. I have read the letter of "Wesleyan" on what he calls a "good old English adjective" with amazement. His condemnation of Rev F H Rayward is most unjust. The word is crude, vulgar, and offensive; and as an expletive is just vile.

Shakespeare uses it chiefly in his play, "King John" – and John was England's worst king. Masefield uses it in "Gallipoli" as part of a quotation. This use does not make a vulgar word "good." A word is not "good" because it is "old as the language." Age only adds to its offensiveness.

Milton did not use it, neither did Wesley. The scholars who translated the Bible into English managed without it. True, the translators made use of a number of crude Saxon words, but their incorporation in Holy Writ does not make them holy. (Their elimination from the Bible is considerably overdue.)

Mr Rayward has done a service to the community. Authors who bawl about liberty must remember Emerson's epigram about recognising an equal right to liberty in others.

JULY NEWS ITEMS

A **conference** representing more than 8,000 **women** members of the Amalgamated Ironworkers and Munitions Workers affirmed support for the equal-pay principle, and resolved to **work untiringly for 100 per cent unionism**. It is not yet clear if the rank-and-file agree.

Various prominent clergy protested against **friendly** refugee aliens being made to work side-by-side with **enemy aliens** by the CCC.

Our shipyards were busy and productive. News item: July 13. Two ships, one for the US Navy, were launched from NSW shipyards yesterday.

The NSW Master Plumbers Association announced that more than **8,000 plumbing jobs** were on their books at the moment. It was expected that many of these might not be serviced for weeks **due to the shortage of manpower and the shortage of steel piping**. It was expected that the list would get longer with time.

Men who are **serving in the armed services may stand for election** on August 21. However, they will not be allowed to campaign wearing their uniforms.

The Australian Red Cross Society has received advice that a **prisoner-of-war camp in Malaya** has acknowledged receipt of food for **48,818 Red Cross parcels**.

It was announced that an **increase of 20 per cent** would be made to the **monthly ration of tobacco**.

You still can't **buy red-and-white striped bull's-eyes**.

July 27ᵗʰ. Maximum prices and profit margins will be fixed for parsnips, turnips, pumpkins, peas, beans, asparagus and sweet potatoes, which are now included in the list of **declared vegetables**.

This means that their **growth and marketing,** by all growers, big and small, will be **controlled by the Government.** Maximum retail prices for all furniture sold by retailers were also set. **The aim was to prevent inflation.**

July 28ᵗʰ. Market gardeners everywhere complained that they **would lose money** if they sold their vegetables **at the new maximums prices** that had been set yesterday.

In the month of **July, remarkable things happened**. The Feds decided that **a number of restrictions** and regulations were no longer necessary, and eased or **removed** them.

The brown-out at night would end **for all areas** south of the Tropic of Capricorn. Keep your household lights on at night. The NES system of wardens would still be retained. **Maybe.**

New rubber tyres would become available for commercial vehicles. **Households would still miss out.**

Masses of textiles were released. Coupons would still be required, but there would be a fair chance that a particular item **would be in stock** when required. **More car parts would be available**. Perhaps your car **can** be repaired after all.

The price of tea would be reduced **by 30 per cent**. More vegetables would be available. **Sales tax on clothing** would be reduced from 12 per cent to 7 per cent. **Six pounds of sugar** per person would be released for the making of jam. The manufacture of **replacement parts for radios** would be re-commenced.

Such changes make you wonder. Just **why did they happen now? Incidentally, the elections** will be held on August 21st.

A woman, aged 28, was found **under a house** in Sydney-suburb Longueville. She had lived there for more than a year unknown to the occupants. She had a malignant growth on her lip and wanted to hide until she died.

A plan to use **Italian prisoners-of-war on farms** to alleviate man-power shortages **was approved** by the Federal Government.

There is talk that some **NES regs will be relaxed**. The NES men might not be required **to roam the streets** so much at night. The name-signs on **railway stations** might be put back. Air-raid wardens might hand in their **gas-masks**. Exciting.

The movie "We'll Meet Again", starring **Vera Lynn** was released. Her song of the same name is still Top of the Pops.

Within the next three months **nylon stockings**, imported from the US under the Lend-Lease agreement, **will be on sale in Australia.**

EARLY ELECTION?

Well, whadda yer know? Stone the crows. Strike a light. Bugger me. Blow me down. You could have knocked me over with a feather. John Curtin **did have an ace up his sleeve**, and he played it at the end of June. He announced the calling of an early Federal election, with August 28th as the tentative date. That left about eight weeks to muster his Party.

The timing of this decision was excellent. His Government was clearly in trouble, with only a slim majority, and he was besieged on all fronts. For example, common sense told him he should have **a National Government**. Then again, beyond that, it was obvious that he was caught in a trap where he wanted to **belt the living daylights out of strikers** but could not because of the power they had over him. On top of that, a few days earlier he had barely **survived a vote of no confidence in Parliament by a single vote**, with the promise of more to come. That was no way to run a government.

A new Parliament, with a true majority, would allow him to control the strikers. He might also get rid of **some of his rat-bag Ministers**, and perhaps ease some of the war-time restrictions. He was no longer pretending that Japanese invasion was imminent, so he could escape from charges that he was deliberately trying to frighten the population for his own political purposes. But above all, if he won the election he could say once and for all that he had **been given a mandate to govern without forming a National Government.**

BIG EVENTS IN ITALY

For the first few weeks in July, the mainland of Italy was bombed. The Italian islands off the coast were the obvious targets, but the major cities right across the nation now also got their share. In Sicily, every day the bombers appeared and dropped their load, and it was pretty obvious that this island was being softened up for an invasion. On the 10th of July, the Allies (largely Canadian and American) launched their first landing, and followed up at different points around the big island over the next few days. To cut a long story short, their subsequent efforts were successful, and by the end of the month, they held the major parts of the island, and were clearly ready to take over the rest. This was a huge fillip for the Allies. Here, at last, the Axis powers were bring routed by the land forces of the capitalist countries, and the Axis powers were looking disconcerted, to say the least.

As part of the bombing of cities, railway marshaling yards in Rome were bombed by the Americans. The British propaganda machine, like the equivalent in Oz, always said that such bombings were "precision" and "targeted" to avoid citizens and non-defence sites. Be this as it may, bombs fell elsewhere, and the Basilica on San Lorenzo near the Vatican was "damaged" on July 25th. The Pope wrote a strong letter condemning this to a high Church official, and this Letter was reported in the newspapers and on Vatican Radio.

All of this might have passed without notice in Oz, except that the leader of the Catholic Church in Australia,

Archbishop Norman Gilroy, came out strongly defending the property of the Church in Rome.

His letter got a huge response.

Letters, C D W. One read with a certain amount of amazement the text of the cable sent by Archbishop Gilroy to the Papal Secretary of State. The words "this dark and tragic hour" come strangely from a citizen of the British Commonwealth of Nations, as one would have thought the bombing of Canterbury, London, and the thousands of religious buildings in the British Isles would have been the time for the use of such words, not the occasion of the bombing of a foreign Fascist capital.

I remember no words of condemnation being used by the Archbishop when Italian airmen had the "honour" of bombing London. Is one to assume that religious buildings in the centre of our Empire are less important than the Basilica of San Lorenzo?

The bombing may to the Archbishop's mind, be an "outrage," but surely there should be some qualification of this statement. It is an "outrage" that the Italian people, the race of which the Pope is a member, should have political leaders who, rather than declare Rome an "**open city**," have exposed it to bombing attacks. If the Italians value their buildings as much as non-nationals apparently do, they have been shown the way to save them for posterity. Rome could be as safe from bombing as the Vatican State.

Letters, J Auld, President, Council of Churches, NSW. All right-thinking people surely deplore the sad fact that in this 20th century methods of waging war that cause wholesale destruction of innocent peaceful people; and of magnificent buildings valued because of centuries of historical sentiment associated with them.

The bombing of Rome by the American Air Force has called forth vehement protests from the Pope and from the Roman Catholic Archbishop of Sydney. They seem to forget the wholesale destruction of cathedrals and churches and many other centres of Christian culture and civilisation in England and Scotland, and many parts of the Continent of Europe. There are other places than Rome that have just as sacred associations for Christian people. In any case, it appears from the latest reports that the destruction of sacred places in Rome has been greatly exaggerated, and those who planned the bombing of that city had given careful instruction to the bombers not to do damage to any but military targets, a view that is evidently accepted by Archbishop Duhig, of Brisbane.

It is not in a spirit of vengeance that the bombing of Rome has been carried out by the Allied leaders, but purely because of military necessity. Their aim is surely to win the war and bring peace to this world, and to do it in the quickest possible time. Towards this end, they rightly judged that one of the most effective ways is to destroy all places that are of military value to the enemy, whether they be in Rome or in any other city. We assuredly all hope that the time is not far distant when this necessary destruction will have come to an end.

Letters, W Lewis. As far as my memory serves me, I cannot recall reading any protest from the Pope, Archbishop Gilroy, or any of the heads of their Church, against either the rape of Ethiopia, or the diabolical use of poison gas. If the bombing of London, in which the Italians asked to take a part, had drawn a protest from the Archbishop, his present protest would deserve more sympathy and consideration.

Comment. The Editor of the *SMH* advised that the volume of Letters was so great that only a sample could be published, and that correspondence on the matter had now been closed. There was no Letter published that supported the Archbishop.

After the initial bombing of Rome, up till the end of the month, it was reported that 100,000 people left Rome for diverse destinations.

A BOMBSHELL FROM MUSSOLINI

On the 27th of the month, the King of Italy, Victor Emmanuel, summoned Mussolini to his presence, and prevailed on him to **resign as head of the Fascist Party and of the Government**. The King appointed Marshal Badoglio as Prime Minister.

It was reported from Rome and adjacent countries that Badoglio immediately took over, and within a few hours had proclaimed that a national curfew would extend from dusk to dawn, and that assemblies of more than three adults in public or private was forbidden. Also, such measures as banning the use of automobiles, motor boats, and aircraft were decreed, and highways and roads were to be kept open. The army was to enforce these rules, and it was free to use the force of arms. A stunned Mussolini and several of his Fascist henchmen were sent away, probably to the Alps, "for their protection."

At the end of the month, the situation in Italy was chaotic. There was virtually no reliable news coming from official sources, though the amount of speculation from everywhere was enormous. A few things though were certain. Mussolini had been toppled, and Italy would continue to fight the war.

Then, as if the situation was not confused enough, the Germans added to the drama. On July 31ˢᵗ, their troops entered the north of Italy from a number of points. This was not at the invitation of the Italians, so it might be construed as an invasion. Or it might just be seen as a friendly ally providing aid to a neighbor in need. No one knew how to take it. In some regions, the resident Italian troops resisted the Germans by force. In some places, they were welcomed. It was all very confusing. We will wait to see what develops when some reliable news filters out.

Overall, the situation in Italy was a delightful change for the allies. The biggest question of all was whether the changed situation would result in the Italians suing for peace. The Allies let it be known that they would accept nothing less that **unconditional surrender**, but what would happen if the Italians really wanted out of the war, was by no means certain. Again, we will have to wait and see.

PRODUCTION BEFORE PRINCIPLE

You will remember that last month a dozen women in a factory employing 1,000 people refused to join a union, and that the other workers closed the factory because of that. Well finally, after six weeks, this situation was resolved.

The Commonwealth was the major customer of the factory. Mid-way though July, it decided that the product of the factory was needed, and told the factory owners that they either re-started making the product or they would lose their contract. The owners (identified at last as Duly and Hansford) could not afford to suffer this loss, and withdrew their support for the dozen non-unionists. They were told they would **have to volunteer to leave, or the factory would be closed.**

This decision by Duly was apparently reluctantly made. They had supported the non-union position throughout, despite the pain, because they rejected the notion that all workers had to join a union. In any case, the dozen women decided that the common welfare of the workers would suffer if the factory was closed, and they "sought relief from their positions". Man-power said they would find work for them at other sites that would not require them to join a union. So the matter was settled.

In leaving, they summed up their position thus:

"We have had hundreds of letters encouraging us in our fight against oppression, in our fight that had as its end the elimination of strikes during war-time, in our fight for greater and continuous concentration on production, and in our fight for that precious jewel of individual freedom. In yielding and saying to the employers we will not join a union, but will efface ourselves and will take our releases in order that your front shop may open and your annexe go ahead, and in forsaking the principles for which we have stood, and in thereby allowing the law of the union to override the law of the land, are we doing what is right?

"By asking for these releases we allow production to continue – how vital in the front shop it is has been pressed upon us. That this argument has no effect with the Government or the strikers is all too apparent. Can we allow it to pass unheeded? We have done in the annexe all we could to keep production going there. Loyally with us have worked 40 others – staff and otherwise. We have worked 10½ hours a day and production has been the best the factory has seen. This, however, gives no assistance to the front shop problem.

The course, therefore, that remains open to us, it seems, is to place **production before principle.** This we have decided to do, and to ask for our releases."

Comment. The whole affair had become a test-case for compulsory unionism. Could a small group of determined people buck the power of the unions? In fact, could anything buck that power, other than a strong Government? **The answer to the first question** appeared, at this moment, to be "no". **The answer to the second question** appeared to be that there was no hope of finding out with an election in the offing.

ALIENS AND REFUGEES

Italians' will to fight. Over the last few years, the Italian army had been associated with some spectacular defeats, and vast numbers of them had been taken as prisoners-of-war. Our own propaganda machines had of course exaggerated this and now the notion commonly held was that **the Italians were poor soldiers, verging on cowardice. This was not at all true**, but they did have a viewpoint that this Letter presents partially.

Letters, P Sonnino. As an Italian anti-Fascist, who has left his country in order to fight the Fascists, I have been appalled by the stupidity of a propaganda that, instead of telling the Italian soldiers how right they are in refusing to fight somebody else's war, insisted on "shamming them into in." Talk of the cowardice of the "Dagoes," when not discarded by a reader as too obvious propaganda, leads to dangerous under-estimation of the foe.

The truth is that Italians, by the criminal madness of Mussolini and his gang, have been put into a hopeless position, when at heart they do not want to fight for the Fascists but, materially, cannot revolt against them. If they resist an invasion, it will be because an organised army has an entity apart from the feelings of its soldiers as individuals.

Twenty years of Fascism have opiated the political conscience of the Italian people, especially of the youngsters. King Victor Emmanuel, the Royal Prince, Marshal Badoglio, are all reactionary figures so deeply associated with Fascism as to be hardly worth mentioning, let alone building upon them more wishful thinking. Practical help to an invading army, necessarily of limited scope, can only come from the Italian underground movements, which, amongst unspeakable difficulties, have kindled the flame of freedom.

Comment. It seems to me that the average Italian soldier was not at all jingoist. He had no aspirations of international empire, he had no love at all for Germany's ambitions, and he had no desire to fight on foreign lands. He was drafted reluctantly into the army, and sent to north Africa to fight for a cause that had no appeal to him. When he got a chance to surrender, to survive, he was happy to do so in preference to the alternative.

Now, however, his homeland was under attack, from the Allies, and perhaps from the Germans. I would expect that his efforts to **defend his family and society** from these aggressors will prove him to be as determined and courageous as any of his adversaries.

MIGRANT MATTERS

Letters, Migrant. Mr M Rathbone's letter reveals a misunderstanding of the standard of the European immigrants who came to this country pre-war. There were certainly some who paid a stiff boat fare and had cash in their pocket, but Mr Rathbone obviously overlooks the fact that **most of them got their fares paid by aid committees, and had their landing money, which everybody was required to produce, lent by those committees.**

The department in Canberra chose immigrants who were able to produce big landing money in preference to others less fortunate. Australia became known for that reason as **the country with the big entrance fee.** Many a less fortunate migrant had to look for other possibilities of emigration, like the United States and South America, where immigration was not depending on landing money.

Letters, A Robson, Legion of Christian Reconstruction, Sydney. After careful selection by the Government from more than ten times their number, European refugees from Nazi persecution were admitted to Australia just before war broke out. Since their arrival in Australia I can say from knowledge that they have done their utmost to serve the country which has given them asylum. The **percentage of refugee aliens volunteering for the armed services has been much higher than the percentage of Australians offering** for service. And yet some people say that these people are sheltering behind our own men who are doing the fighting on their behalf. They have, in fact, suffered at the hands of Hitler – long before we ever thought of war.

The irony of fate now is that our authorities should send them to work in camps **side by side with aliens with strong Nazi sympathies, whose brothers are at**

present persecuting the families and relations of these same refugee aliens; and they are expected to be happy and to work harmoniously side by side in the same camp. In these camps it is proposed to break down labour conditions by undercutting award rates, if the foreman thinks that a full job is not being done. Would any Australian stand for such arbitrary undercutting of his own or his mate's rates? To send highly skilled professional men to such camps to work on road-making, or some similar project, is a scandalous waste of talent and training. And it does seem inhuman to send medically unfit men to hard labouring work where there is bound to be inadequate medical and hospital attention. I feel certain that average Australian public opinion is not behind the action being taken this week by the authorities. Why then is it being done?

OTHER MATTERS

Letters, Butcher. The reason 70 per cent of the master butchers are with the men in wanting the Wednesday half-holiday is on account of the extra work placed on owners and men. I am 59 years of age and got the medically unfit badge from the last big war. I have been serving in my shop ever since, and am called upon to stand and serve from 8 a.m. till 5.30 Monday to Friday. On Saturday I have to start at 2 a.m. and finish 1 p.m., which is a full day's work, so we really work a full day on Saturday, therefore getting no half-day.

The men start at 3 or 4 o'clock so as to get the work ready for opening time. I lost my three men, two joining the AIF (one my own son) and the other taken by the Militia. By closing at 12.30 on Wednesday, I have a chance of remaining in business.

Letters, Ransome T Wyatt, Goulburn. "A C" did not go back far enough into history with his story of the arrest of marauding goats in Goulburn. In 1876, the goat nuisance was so bad in Goulburn that the PM called a meeting of magistrates to ascertain if the minimum fine of 10/- could be increased to 1 Pound. Thirteen years later, the police tackled the problem, rounding up and destroying 24 in North Goulburn alone.

Letters, Unfair. Recently two boxers came from Melbourne, two week-ends in succession, and earned money. I was nursing in the last war and now do a lot of voluntary work, yet when I applied recently to go to Melbourne to recuperate after an illness my application was not granted. Why give boxers priority?

Letters, One Shiverer. Have the authorities fairly considered the severe discomforts that arise from the prohibition on the use of coke for household heating? If fuel is short it should be rationed on a proper basis, especially where families are suffering from 'flu and colds.

Letters, M S. Mr Evatt suggests what I would describe as beach wear for school children. As a mother of six, and having had years of experience with children, give me the uniform. The children realize it is school they are dressed for, and not play. Therefore, we must dress our children accordingly. What I pay for a tunic to last the year is nothing compared with the expense of a number of frocks and extra underwear that would be needed, to say nothing of the labour.

Letters, T Dunn Sir Earle Page and Mr Scully appear at variance over the food shortage. Could I suggest that they leave the farmers alone, and look nearer home for wastage. Potatoes were wasted at Christmas time: they should have been either tinned or pitted. I have seen many tons of potatoes **pitted** in Crookwell in the early days, but it appears a lost art. As for mouldy cheese, with reasonable care, cheese will keep almost indefinitely. We used to make cheese all the summer before refrigeration was available, and sell during the winter without any losses.

Letters, Fair Go. When the Commonwealth Government needed pigeons for their war work, we fanciers gave them of our best willingly. Is it asking too much of them to release the small amount of manpower necessary for the making of aluminium rings? A pigeon without this aluminium band is useless, as one has no record of its age, breeding, etc., and unless some provision is made, many fanciers will not breed at all this season, to the detriment of a very valuable hobby.

Letters, M Rathbone. A thrice-weekly delivery of ice to homes would be more than ample if people were to treat their ice-chests properly. The chest should be placed in a dark corner where there is absolutely no draught. The ice should not be wrapped in paper or anything else. A thick blanket or rug should be thrown over the chest, especially on hot days. By this method food is cooler, ice lasts longer, and there is less drip-water to be emptied.

AUGUST NEWS ITEMS

Over the last week, Allied bombing of the German port of Hamburg has destroyed much of the city. 400,000 have become refugees (out of a total population of 1,200,000).

Goebells has ordered the evacuation of all children and non-essential adults from Berlin, as a precaution against raids similar to those on Hamburg.

Many retailers are refusing to sell potatoes because they say that the maximum price fixed is too low. They were currently being sold in cities at a loss of one shilling a bag.

A free private-car service to provide transport for expectant mothers from their homes to hospitals has been organised in North Sydney. So far, 22 people have offered their cars to the service for six suburbs.

Additional labour will be made available to enable employees in Sydney and Newcastle and other cities' tram and bus services to take three days off per month and two weeks annual leave.

Within the next three months nylon stockings, imported from the US under the Lend-Lease agreement, will be on sale in Australia.

In the first few months of 1943, a newly-created Women's Employment Board made some rulings. One of these was that female wages should be paid at about 90 per cent of the male rate for nearly equivalent work. Employers objected on the grounds that such a move would send them broke.

In mid-August, the High Court brought down the decision that the above ruling was valid in law.

A day later, the ACTU advised 73 Federal Unions, who have members employed under awards made by the Board, to make claims for back-pay due. Turmoil.

August 17th, Tuesday. The Federal elections will be held **next Saturday.** The eight national and commercial radio stations in Sydney will broadcast **74 election talks today and tomorrow**. After that, **no broadcasts will be permitted**.

Commonwealth Officers raided an industrial plant which has been supplying an **extensive black market with hair oil and cosmetics.** How the plant's operators came to **possess large stocks** of corks, many types of bottles, and hundreds of cartons **is being investigated**.

Damien Parer, famous Australian War photographer, is on his way home **from New Guinea with 3,000 feet of film,** which he believes contains some of the best footage he has ever shot.

President Roosevelt has issued **an order to prevent strikes in the US war industries.** Penalties are prescribed for both unions and employers. Oz is not the only place with strikes.

The importation, production and distribution of **internal combustion engines** will be placed under **the control of a Committee,** based in Canberra. Its powers will apply to **all car engines.** A similar Committee will be set up to control all aspects of **trade in chocolate, cocoa and confectionery**.

THE ELECTIONS

The big exciting day was August 21. Before that, the candidates had stumped round the nation, addressing audiences at town halls, in their workplaces, off the backs of trucks in the streets, and via the radio. They had placed a ton of newspaper ads, and put up a million posters, though these mostly stuck to **the size restrictions**. The rallies were jolly good fun, punch-ups were rare, many of the speakers could be heard and many could not and, I believe, not a single person, who tried to listen, changed their voting intentions.

PERSONAL MEMORY. As an aside, I can remember walking from my home town of Abermain to Chinaman's Hollow in the next town, with a crowd of one hundred voters. This march was a torchlight procession, where about twenty men carried burning kerosene torches blazing over their heads to light the way. We were stopped on the way by a warden who told us to put out those lights, but some union muscle told him to go away. At the cricket ground, half a dozen speakers gave us the message. This was a 100 per cent coal-mining community, so the message was that the Labour Government was great, the unions were somehow also great, that Communism was pretty good, Bob Menzies was a bastard, and any one who thought differently was a scab. And, to coin a deservedly-famous quote, we all went home tired but happy.

Back to the elections. The Opposition Party was in chaos. It was a coalition of two Parties, the Country and the United Party. The first of these was led by Arthur Fadden, but he made some silly promises and attracted no uncommitted voters to his Party.

The United Party was led by William Morris Hughes, known as Billie, the Little Digger, who was a veteran politician from WWI. He was shadow of his former self, and spent most of his time snapping at the heels of the Government. That means he had no new policies to excite the voters. Even worse, just two months ago, the Party was split into two roughly-equal halves, when many members tried to unseat Hughes in favour of Bob Menzies. They failed in this, but the losers formed a "cave" that said they were going to try again. So the United Party was hopelessly split.

Could the Labour Party take advantage of the weakness of the Opposition? Well, maybe. If you take the bigger picture, and look back at the last 18 months, Labour had somehow mobilised the nation, got its manpower working in essential industries on major construction projects, got most of its servicemen back to Australia, and had done its share in turning the Japanese round. What a fantastic 18 months. First, indecision, then out-right fear, then uncertainty, and now complete confidence in the outcome. Could you throw out a Government that had done all this?

Well, again maybe. If you come down to detail, there were some bad bits. Rationing to "feed Britain", stupid regulations and stupid Ministers, the compulsory sending of our troops overseas, the failure to take on the strikers. The list of complaints could go on and on. Were they enough to unseat a government?

The deciding factor was John Curtin, and his able Treasurer, Ben Chifley. Curtin in particular, through all the tribulations and uncertainties, had held his nerve and done the right thing for the nation. His hand had been steady, his actions moderate, and the results were now **triumphantly successful**. He had had his problems, such as his fight with Churchill over the disposition of Oz troops. He had had more problems, such as curbing his maverick Ministers. But he had remained dedicated to the cause of winning the war, and worked at that every day till he just about dropped. He and Chifley were held in the highest regard by the Press, most other politicians, and inevitably the people. Together, this pair could be an election winner.

I enclose a smattering of Letters that cover various aspects of the campaign.

Letters, R Clive Teece. Under the heading "Dr Evatt ends an argument", a Labour Party announcement, appears this statement by Dr Evatt (Labour): "Under Labour Government there will be **more room for private enterprise and business initiative after the war than ever before**." So far from ending an argument, no statement is better calculated to begin an argument – an argument between Dr Evatt on the one hand and Messrs Curtin, Beasley, Ward, and other Labour stalwarts on the other hand – men pledged to bring into effect the Labour platform of the "socialisation of industry, production, distribution, and exchange."

How the extension of private enterprise and business initiative is to be reconciled with the socialisation of industry, production, distribution, and exchange will require a great deal of argument.

Letters, T J Butler. Communists seem to be the catspaw, or one of them, of politics. When their candidates are eliminated in the counting of votes, their first preferences always go to the Labour candidates, so the result is precisely the same as if the Communists voted No. 1 Labour in the first place. Yet the Prime Minister seems to think it is a good idea to advertise in all papers all over the Commonwealth that there is no alliance between Labour and Communism.

Letters, G Haskins. The conduct of this election campaign is undermining the morale of the electors. Election speeches, with certain notable exceptions such as those by Dr Evatt and Mr Spooner, seem to consist mainly of bitter denunciation of the work and achievements of the other party. There is little that is constructive, and I feel under grave doubt as to how to record my vote.

I certainly will not give it to the candidate who can do no better for his country than to rail at his political opponents.

Mr Curtin may have been a pre-war pacifist, but at least his great effort in this war is worthy of the commendation of the nation. Why not judge him on the war work he has done rather than his alleged expressed view prior to this war? There is a clear case for a national Government, composed of earnest men who will guide us to victory and thereafter to wise reconstruction, but how as electors can we ensure this?

Perhaps the solution may be to support any worthy candidate with a constructive aim and mind, who is prepared to work for a national Government, and who, moreover, will not follow the foolish, ungenerous, and petty method of electioneering which unhappily is now so rampant.

Letters, William Lock. The notification that Dr Evatt will speak at Double Bay on **Sunday night** in support of the endorsed Labour candidate will shock a great number of patriotic citizens. The holding of **political**

meetings on the Lord's Day contravenes the purpose for which the day is designed, namely that of rest and worship. The splendid service rendered to the Empire by Dr Evatt is appreciated. It must be emphasised, however, that in the highest interests of the Empire and civilisation, it is essential to build upon the foundations, which are moral and spiritual.

Letters, F McClean, Lt.-Col., 1ˢᵗ AIF. In Thursday's "Herald" you publish a photograph of Mr Fadden addressing a political meeting at Fivedock, with the Union Jack draping a table on the platform. This is most improper. **The Jack should be flown**, not used to cover a table. I submit that the use of the Union Jack in this manner is illegal, and, although it is a common practice in this country, it should be stopped.

Letters, G Holt. An old man keenly interested in politics, for the first time in his life, does not know how to vote! I live in the Barton Division, and was very pleased when I was able to cast a vote for Dr Evatt at the last election, for he is the one man in the political life of Australia who resigned a high, dignified position, with a big salary and a pension, to enter into the hurly-burly of politics. Since he has been in Parliament he has done well, become a senior Minister, has gone to the USA and Britain twice in the service of Australia. Surely he is a man to vote for. And yet I believe in a National Government. Dr Evatt is a member of a Government that does not. When Mr Churchill was called upon to form a Ministry, aristocrat though he is, with a party majority behind him, he went to the brains of the House to form his Government. But Mr Curtin forms a party Government in which he has to find a Speaker from his opponents and have a majority of one, an independent. And what was his Ministry like? One brilliant man, Dr Evatt, three able men, himself and Messrs Chifley and Beasley, a number of mediocrities and at least two political absurdities. A vote for Dr Evatt means a vote in favour of that Government. I believe in trade unions, but I do not believe in compelling every one that works to join a union, and I don't believe the trade unions should control the Government, which is what seems to be happening lately. How shall I vote? If I vote against Dr Evatt, whom I believe to be one of the best four men in politics, I vote in favour of things I detest.

Letters, "Ukalunda". No Australian political party has any claim on having "saved Australia." The "Herald" was alone in advocating armament from the time of the Lyons Government until the war broke out. But neither the Menzies Government nor Labour were much concerned about armament. Then we sent divisions abroad to fight alongside the Motherland, but Britain armed them, not Australia. Our politicians looked at the war from a distance like spectators at a stage drama, and the Government was "detached." This attitude was antagonistic to armament up to the time when the Curtin Government gained office by the aid of "independents" (who were not independent).

Pearl Harbour and Malaya cast a bomb on the political sweets of office. Like an antbed stirred with a stick, Ministers had to volte-face on their traditional policy, and get to work to seriously arm Australia. Any other Government would have done the same. **The real saviours of this fair land of ours are America and, in a lesser degree, Britain.** Our need is a National Government free from party politics, and one that will give "credit where credit is due."

The election result. I must try for some drama here. A few of you will already know the result. But we delay while the votes are counted, so we will wait to Page 111 when all will be revealed.

DAYLIGHT SAVING

Although its popularity with the States came and went, at the moment most Oz States were prepared to introduce it for the next year. Not everyone liked the idea.

Letters, Edward Boyd. If daylight saving is banned during the coming summer, backyard vegetable growing will slump. Satisfactory results cannot be obtained from weekend gardening only; but with one hour in the garden each evening during the warm half of the year, ample yields of vegetables can be obtained. It is the watering, spraying, and dusting **each evening** which ensures the obtaining of good crops, and especially with tomatoes.

Letters, P Cleak. May I point out the enormous saving in electrical energy which will be the result of daylight saving? By adopting it, street, house, and shop lighting will be curtailed by one hour. If not accepted, it will be a **crime against the war effort** and other contingencies. Accordingly it is our bounden duty to introduce daylight-saving, even if in some instances it may mean a personal sacrifice.

Letters, Truth. Incorrect suggestions have been made by correspondents – **One.** Light and power are saved by daylight saving; **Two**. It assists the home agriculturist. Daylight saving is contrary to the wishes of more than 80 per cent of the people, is very trying, tiring, uncalled-for, wasteful, and of negative effect upon the war effort.

Letters, A Mother of Seven Young Australians. If daylight saving would end the war a day earlier, mothers would put up with any sacrifice it would entail, but will it? As for the gentleman with the pencil and paper who worked out the saving in coal as 2d a head, I say, "fiddlesticks." After the heat of our Australian summer days, children simply go to bed an hour later at no saving in electricity. After carrying heavy loads of provisions from the shops, and without any assistance in the home, even at the wash tub, a mother longs for the end of the day when, children in bed, she can relax and have a little time to herself. Daylight saving robs her of a precious hour of this short period for relaxation.

Letters, Martha Grimsley. Daylight saving is cruel to old people who have had to bear the heat of a long, hot day. They cannot sleep when they go to bed, the rooms still being hot. The children are out in the streets until all hours, so no one gets any benefit out of daylight saving. Let us keep to the old way. I suggest that anyone who wants the extra time for gardening should get up that hour earlier, and do it in the morning.

There were others who welcomed the change.

Letters, Bruce Ashby. For years, the kookaburras have burst out laughing about an hour before dawn. Under daylight saving, they still laugh one hour before dawn. That is despite the fact that dawn comes an hour earlier every day. But somehow they know this. How can this be? There can be no other possible explanation other than divine control. Surely this is just one more proof of the existence of God.

Mr Conrad, below, had analysed the matter, and came up with a well reasoned argument **against**.

Letters, Nigel Conrad. When daylight-saving is imposed on us, I lose one hour's sleep at the beginning. Then every night for about five months, I lose another one hour. That adds up at the end to about 150 hours. Then, at the end of saving, I get one hour back. Just one. That means that over those months, I lose about 150 hours.

Suppose I do this for 60 years. I will lose about 9,000 hours of sleep. No wonder old people do not move as fast and are always tired. They are exhausted.

So let me make a plea to any leaders who are young enough to still be intelligent. Get rid of day-light saving, and rejuvenate the nation.

But these leaders should go a step further. Instead of taking away an hour's sleep at the beginning, move the clocks **back** an hour. Then we get an extra hour's sleep on the first night, and so on for the entire season. You can see how much sleep we will **gain** over the season, and that will of course flow through to older people, who will be restored to the vigour of their childhood.

Comment. Over many years, I have seen daylight saving come and go. The arguments for and against, though, remain about the same. Those for it say that you get more drinking time, the hens lay more eggs, or the roosters lay more. Those against it say it fades the curtains, they are always tired, the cows won't let down their milk, and the cane toads breed more.

The best argument I have heard against it is the one from Nigel Conrad above. Based on sound irrefutable arithmetic, he not only points to the biological imperative involved, but provides a useful way of working **with** nature to benefit mankind. If ever I move to the position of Dictator of Australia, the first policy I will introduce will be his of "daylight losing." In fact, I will go one step further, and introduce it **all year round**. Then, everyone can reap the benefits, not just for four months of the year, but for the entire year.

A NATIONAL ANTHEM

Letters, Alex Burnard. It is a natural and healthy thing, that many people of our young, self-aware nation are "taking thought" about their own national song. I stress at the outset that there is no question of abrogating, or even competing with "God Save the King." That is a consummate tune of its type; by its forthrightness and dignity giving us the British genius and character. Tradition, respect, and love ensure its retention.

Letters, Tom Murphy. Advance Australia Fair. This little "occasional piece," written frankly for a school break-up, is expected to mix and rub shoulders with better music. I weigh words carefully – and my fellow-musicians will be with me, I fancy – when I say that this tune is a pinchbeck hotch-potch, and that no amount of "plugging," folating and fobbing will make it represent us as a nation any more than the current explosive "Hiya, Folks," and similar fashions of a year represent the American soul and nation.

Some months ago, after an important international broadcast the British and American anthems were played, and after them this pathetic poor relation. It was from righteous wrath and not a trace of snobbishness, that we writhed at the contrast and the blow to our pride.

"The Song of Australia" – written long before the local claimant was sired – is still hale and beloved by those who know it well, and is worthy of us in both tune and words.

Comment. A number of people suggested the "Song of Australia", written by an English woman, Caroline Carlton, who came to Oz in 1839.

The first verse goes:

> There is a land where summer skies
> Are gleaming with a thousand dyes,
> Blending in witching harmonies, in harmonies;
> And grassy knoll, and forest height,
> Are flushing in the rosy light,
> And all above in azure bright -
> Australia!

Letters, J Johnstone. I was surprised to hear a statement during the State programme of the ABC to the effect that "Advance Australia Fair" is generally considered to be Australia's National Anthem. This is manifestly incorrect. Possessing as we do a hymn to Almighty God which expresses our national faith as well as our loyalty to our Sovereign under God, what good reason can any loyal subject have for seeking some other song to be our National Anthem?

ELECTION RESULTS

Labour romped it in, winning about a dozen extra seats in the House of Reps. In the Senate, it also did well and, from now on, it need not be worried about being voted down, and out.

For Curtin, this was a great result. Now, probably, people would stop carping on about forming a National Government. He could henceforth say that he was now **given a mandate by the people for single-Party government.** In any case, he could argue, his government had seen the Japanese hordes turned around and in retreat, without a National government. Why would we want one now?

He was also in a position to shift some of his cowboy ministers. He had only an indirect say in this, because it was **the Labour Caucus that decided who was to be a minister**. But this same Caucus had to listen to a Prime Minister whose party had won such a splendid electoral victory, so he would have more control of who did what than ever before.

One point of interest is that, for the first time, women were elected to Parliament. One, a 30-year old teacher from Western Australia, went to the Senate. The second, the well-known Enid Lyons, also went to Canberra.

Comment. It seems to me to be a sensible result. It remains to be seen if the new Government would come to grips with the strike menace.

RAILWAY STRIKE IN THE US

In America, a railway dispute has resulted in **Roosevelt ordering Government possession and control of all railway companies.** He said the action was necessary to ensure the movement of troops and war materials.

He announced later that he intends to retain control and ownership of the railways **only so long as the strikes in the industry continues. A novel attempt at strike-breaking.** We will wait to see how effective it works out to be.

SEPTEMBER NEWS ITEMS

At the start of the month, the wheels were starting to fall off the German dominance of Europe. **Victory in Sicily had recently been won. But the other conquered nations were getting restless, even defiant.**

In Denmark, there was continued resistance by the Danes, who had resorted to strikes, civil disobedience, and actual open warfare.

In Bulgaria, observers say that anarchy will take over unless Germany fully takes over the country, or the Allies take the opportunity to attack on that flank in Europe.

In France, there was a rising tide of sabotage. **In neutral Sweden**, Oslo Radio (under German control) admitted a "widespread enemy sabotage network"

September 1st. **In Sydney yesterday**, the first Manpower **call-up from the taxi industry was made**. 160 drivers were diverted to other industries. More drivers will be reviewed tomorrow.

A warning from the Security Services was issued. It reminded the population that scores of **letter-writers, writing privately to friends and families**, were summoned each week for interviews. In most cases, a reprimand and a warning were issued as sufficient deterrents. **Censorship rules within the nation were still being fully enforced**, including the opening and reading of random letters.

Letters to prisoners and internees in Japanese hands **must in future be limited to 25 words**, and must be typed or written in block letters. This is because of demands by Japanese authorities who have to censor each letter.

The Federal Government has decreed that all **hamburger shops and all-night cafes must close at midnight** to prevent "undesirables" from picking up Servicemen.

September 10th. New **regulations** issued last night **banning** any member, or former member, of **the defence forces** from **divulging information** reaching him through his service. **Don't mention the war.** This would prohibit, for example, a returned soldier from reporting faults to his local Member or to complaints bodies. Papers, using enforced wartime restraint, described the Regs as **"drastic".**

September 14th. The Prime Minister indicated that the new **security regulations**, described above, were immediately **revoked**. He said that they had been introduced by Public Servants, directed by **John Dedman**, without Curtin's knowledge. He indicated that current Regs covered such matters fully. Such **dithering at the top level** did little to inspire confidence in Government.

The Minister for the Army announced that **170 doctors had been released from serving in the Army** recently.

Again. **Lest We Forget. The War goes on.** A **casualty list of 954 names** was issued by the Army. In the list, 877 men who had previously been listed as missing were now reported as **prisoners of war**.

In mid-September, there were **5,000 Italian prisoners-of-war in Australia.** Don't ask me how they got here. Also, there were 2,023 Australian prisoners in Italy.

There was a **big rush to join the Waterside Union** by persons trying to establish that they are **workers in a protected industry**. Tickets would, however, only be issued to persons known to the Union. Many tickets were being issued to the relatives of existing members. **Manpower** is having an effect, though probably **not what it wanted**.

Passengers should be able **to travel to England in 60 hours**, after the War, said Qantas.

The Chairman of the NSW Housing Commission said that NSW had **80,000 fewer houses than it needed**.

The Department of Health said today that **Australians eat too much meat**. It claimed that 4 ounces of meat per day was sufficient to keep adults in good health. **No mention was made of rationing in the future,** but cynics thought that this might be the start of a softening up process.

The American Armed Services Band of 80 members marched in the main streets of Sydney. They were given a reception at the Town Hall. They will give a concert there tonight.

A **small-scale civil war** has broken out between two separate **guerilla** organisations in Greece. This set the pattern for other countries in the future. As the guerillas evolved, the **Communists** sought to get power, and an opposing ideology tried to stop them.

For example, Tito in Yugoslavia.

ITALY IN TROUBLE

Things moved quickly in the month of September in Italy. The Allies, after cleaning up in the island of Sicily, invaded the south of the mainland, and pushed northwards without much early resistance. After a few days of this, the new President of Italy, Badoglio, formally surrendered unconditionally. He ordered Italian troops to lay down their arms, and it seems they were mostly very glad to do this.

That, however, did not mean the end of fighting there. The Germans were now in position to take over the defence of the nation, and soon were providing a strong defence of Naples. However, the hinterland round Naples gradually fell to the Allies and at the end of the month it seemed that nothing could save that city.

For the Allies, and the opponents of Nazism worldwide, the successful invasion of South Italy was very grand indeed. Here at last, the Axis powers were on the run in their own lands. This was great for morale, and it encouraged guerilla movements, particularly in the Balkans, to expand their activities. In some areas, for example, on the coast of Yugoslavia, the patriots there came into **open conflict** with their German occupiers, and showed that the Germans could be beaten by hit-and-run tactics.

So, the events in Italy were a great fillip for the propaganda machines of the Allies. But Hitler was not nearly finished, and he pulled off a propaganda coup of his own.

OTTO SKORZENY

Mussolini was being held as a prisoner in a hotel near the top of Gran Sasso, the highest peak in the Appenines range of mountains, 100 miles from Rome. **Hitler decided to rescue him**. To do that, he enlisted an Austrian dare-devil and adventurer called Otto Skorzeny. This gentleman decided that to go in by road would be fatal, and that using parachutes would be risky and uncertain.

So, on September 12th, he and 107 men boarded gliders and headed for Mussolini's hotel. Mussolini was quietly contemplating suicide, when the gliders swanned in and landed within 100 yards of the hotel. The Carabinieri and military guards were caught unawares as the marauders took control, and surrendered with only a few scuffles. Mussolini was bustled into a light aircraft that had accompanied the marauders, and flew out to safety in Vienna. The rest of the raiders escaped by using **a routine cable-car down from the mountains.**

This most daring raid gave Hitler a magnificent chance to strut his stuff. Needless to say, he got maximum propaganda coverage from it. As for Mussolini, he went on to visit Hitler two days later, and was reluctantly persuaded to resume his former role as leader of the nation. He took to the airwaves, saying he was back, and ordering the arrest of anyone associated with his confinement. He moved to Milan, in the north of Italy, and **set up a puppet government**, trying to revive the now-disbanded Fascist Party.

Italy was now in complete chaos. The Allied troops had been greeted with great joy wherever they landed. But the German troops now quickly took over from the Italians and, within weeks, had control, more or less, of the northern part of the nation. The Italian army could not work out whether to support Germany, or to fight it. Mostly, it wanted to surrender, and put down its arms.

Over the next few months, **it came to a terrible end**, with 450,000 of them transported to Germany to work as slave labour. **I repeat, 450,000 of them**. Others were even less fortunate. The entire garrison of 8,400 men at Cephalonia, off the coast of Greece, fought the Germans for a week until they ran out of ammunition. The Germans shot them all and burned their corpses.

So, now at the end of September, Italy was in a mess, almost anarchy. Over the next few months, the Allies would press north, to the foot of the Alps, where the Germans held firm during the heavy seasonal rains of Autumn, and then for the snow-bound months of winter. The Italian campaign would, at the start of next year, remain bogged down, and have less significance as the Allies moved towards a Second Front, probably in France.

ZOOT SUITS

The last months of 1943 saw the introduction of **zoot suits** to Australian cities. This wonderful outfit for young men had its origin in the US, where it was originality worn as a protest against the world in general. Young blacks and Mexicans, and those who craved connections with gangsters and the under-world, would flaunt their individuality and aggression through appearing in such suits. There was no chance of missing them.

Malcolm X, well-known for something or other, described them. "I was measured, and the young salesman picked off a rack a zoot suit that was just wild: **sky-blue pants thirty inches in the knee and angle narrowed down to twelve**

inches at the bottom, and a long coat that pinched my waist and flared out below my knees. As a gift, the salesman said, the store would give me a narrow leather belt with my initial 'L' on it. Then he said I ought to also buy a hat, and I did – **blue, with a feather in the four-inch brim**. Then the store gave me another present: a **long, thick-lined, gold plated chain that swung down lower than my coat hem**. I took three of those twenty-five cent sepia-toned, while-you wait pictures of myself, posed the way "hipsters" wearing their zoots would "cool it" – hat angled, knees drawn close together, feet wide apart, both index fingers jabbed toward the floor. The long coat and swinging chain and the Punjab pants were much more dramatic if you stood that way."

Back in Australia, the fashion was introduced to this nation by US soldiers on long-leave. They were quite popular with some girls, and so they crept into the wardrobe of Australian men. However, they were not suitable for everyone. Initially, wearing them, there was always the risk that servicemen in uniform, or even civilians, would see you as being rebels of some sort, and decide you needed a good bashing. As they became more popular, this hazard was reduced, but still the ordinary wharf-labourer or lawyer would not be seen dead in them. They were more for wear by lairs in nightclubs.

Comment. Remember that clothing was rationed, so that those men who respected the law found that they could not afford the volumes of material for their making. I notice that zoot suits are currently available in Oz on the internet.

I suspect that one day they will stage a comeback. Will fun-filled girls still go crazy over them?

THE PERSECUTION OF THE JEWS

Hitler was now moving towards his "final solution" to his "Jewish problem." He had imprisoned millions of them already and now, for many other yellow-star branded citizens, he introduced his solution by sending them to their death in gas chambers. This applied right across his empire, in its most terrible form in Poland. As you all know, several million Jews met their deaths in this way, and billions of dollars worth of property was confiscated. At this time, however, most of the people of Europe knew nothing of the deaths and were surprised after the war to hear of them. Ribbentrop, Hitler's trusted Foreign Minister, at the War Crimes trials at Nuremburg after the war, said they he had never heard of the death camps and doubted that there were any. No one believed him at all, but there were many who were in the same boat that he tried to occupy.

JUVENILE DELINQUENTS: HARSH TREATMENT

Delinquents were the same pain in the neck then as they are today. I will soon show you some Letters and opinions on the problem, but **first I must explain a reference made to the so-called "prison ships" mentioned therein.** For example, the Sobraon was a large sailing ship, built in 1866 as a passenger clipper. She was the "largest composite-hull sailing vessel ever built" and plied the seas between England and Eastern Australia.

From 1891 till 1927, she was used firstly as a "reformatory" ship and a "training ship" for the Australian Navy. Whatever you called it, the idea was that male juvenile delinquents were sent there as punishment for their offences. While there, they were trained in the skills of the sea, and this, it was hoped, would have a rehabilitative effect on them. The ship was anchored well off-shore at Cockatoo Island in Sydney Harbour, and then Rose Bay, to prevent the inmates from escaping by swimming. The ship was broken up in 1941.

Given that background, you are ready for these tough Letters.

Letters, Tam O'Shanter. It is stated in the "Herald" that during **the past year about 300 boys absconded from the Gosford Training School.** It is a problem these days to know how to secure the future well-being of boys who stray from the paths of rectitude, but it was not such a problem 50 years ago, when the training ship Vernon was the standing factor in providing secure conditions governing such cases as are daily reported from the Gosford Training School.

Is it not time that something should be done to re-establish another training ship like the old Vernon, or its successor, the Sobraon, and by so doing lessen 90 per cent of the juvenile crime of today?

Letters, C Turner. "Tam O'Shanter" deplores the wildness of boyhood, and states that there was not such a problem fifty years ago. I beg to differ. I also have a clear memory of the training ship Vernon, and of its reputation for refined brutality. The punishment for desertion was so severe that only the most desperate made the attempt. Whilst at Begg's Siding sawmill during the winter of 1919, it was not unusual for a starveling who had fled from Mittagong to beg food from us. It was useless to point out to the boys that they could not long escape custody. Their hungry looks and despairing yet defiant manner always evoked practical sympathy. I venture the opinion that cruelty to children may harden and brutalise, but will never become a factor of reform.   Children do not flee from kindness and fair dealing.

Letters, Tam O'Shanter.   Your correspondent, Mr Turner, appears to have taken a wrong view of my letter. I did not "deplore the wildness of boyhood," but one may deplore the lack of parental control over boys, necessitating institutions like training schools, for their reception through careless home training. Our present system of training schools is excellent, and boys who conform to discipline – which is in no way harsh – have no reason for absconding in such numbers as reported. They have only to conduct themselves in a reasonable manner, and they receive excellent treatment, but often they mistake kindness for weakness and take advantage of it.

Whatever your correspondent may have heard about the reputation of brutality on the Vernon in days past is no proof of its truth, for I happen to have known Captain Neitenstein personally, who was in charge of that training ship, and a more humane man would be hard to find. The then Government held him in such high esteem that he was subsequently appointed Chief of the Prisons Department, where he earned the respect of everyone, and his innovations of prison reform have been copied by most systems throughout the world. Such was the man who controlled the Vernon, and her successor the old Sobraon, and it speaks volumes for his work there when it has been shown that not one of his boys of either ship has been known to turn out a criminal.

Letters, Just A Teacher. As a matter of fact – while God forbid that the Neitenstein system should ever return – the pendulum has gone to the other extreme and the theorist who knows nothing of the problems has introduced **a namby-pamby sentimentalism that**

shelters under the false label of child-study. The psychologist is examining and re-examining and what is well being brought out is that we have in the child delinquent a result – a result of misunderstanding, mismanagement, heredity, environment, or "what you will". But, because someone else has failed properly to train the child is no reason why the State should fail in its duty and give post-graduate courses in law-breaking and authority defiance by almost winking at the rising numbers of absconders. That the absence of effectual punishment of the absconder is the basic cause is evidenced by the fact that, previous to the passing of the clause making it "an offence" to punish by more than six strokes, the number of absconders annually from Gosford was not more than 20 per cent of present figures. **The writer does not advocate "flogging," a term used whenever physical punishment is suggested, but still believes in an appeal through the skin when other methods have failed – and they are failing daily.**

POST-WAR TALK

Letters, H Blake. All praise to Mr Curtin, and to Mr Hughes, too, for their high resolve that all men of the fighting forces, and all men and women engaged on war work, shall be given jobs when they once again return to civil life. But where are the jobs coming from? All these people can't enter the Civil Service, and jobs don't come out of thin air. Most of them depend upon private enterprise.

It will take time to build many businesses up again, even if the owners possess the capital at the end of the war to do so. The needs of war come first, and no one questions that, but there is no call for harshness in following it out. The Government should keep in mind that times will come when it will have need of all the help private enterprise can give it if the necessary jobs are to materialise.

The retail trade has been the object of much Ministerial derision. One could be led to believe, from the public utterances and threats of some Ministers, that the retail store had no real place in the scheme of things, and was one of the scourges of modern life. Yet the retail trade, directly and indirectly, pays the bulk of the nation's taxes, and again, directly or indirectly, provides most of the nation's employment. Even a Governmental theorist should be able to see its economic place in normal times. Apart from those directly engaged in the retail trade, vast numbers of others employed in manufacture, in transport, and so on are dependent upon it.

Yet today the retail store is being willfully handicapped at every turn. Irritating and countless regulations, many of them without any apparent purpose are thrust upon it; taxes have mounted to alarming heights, and the biggest problem of every store at the moment is how to hang on and continue to function.

MEAT RATIONING COMING SOON

Meat rationing will be introduced in next January. Coupons will be issued to the Oz population, and each person over 9 years of age will receive two-and-a-half pounds of meat per week. Younger children will receive one-and-a-half pounds. Coupons will be issued to allow this. Coupons will also be issued to **household pets** and gaming dogs.

OCTOBER NEWS ITEMS

Oct 1st. The NSW Minister for the NES, Mr Heffron, announced that **boards, wire netting and other materials** over windows could be **removed** if owners wished to do so. He added that labour shortages might make this difficult.

Oct 8th. The Federal Government said that the materials covering windows **could not yet be removed**. People who removed them in the last week would **need to replace them**.

The Fourth Liberty Loan, seeking 125 million Pounds was opened by John Curtin. It is seeking money for the war-effort.

20,000 men would be released by the Services to work on the land. Preference would be given to those with experience with dairy cattle and pigs. Also, 15,000 men will be re-directed from munitions production to other essential work. **30,000 women** will be called up for **"war production."**

Holidays are back. October 4th, then **called Six-Hour Day**, was treated as a normal public holiday, and **workers were generally not expected to work**. The PM said that **miners this year would get a break of nine days at Christmas.**

1,000 Italian prisoners-of-war had arrived in Australia. They will be used to ease the man-power shortage.

The Production Executive in Canberra has recommended that **all dogs in Oz be restricted to eating horse meat** for the duration of the war. This matter has not been passed into legislation.

October 9th. Meat sales will be restricted in most cities of Oz. Butchers will receive about **25 per cent of the normal capacity,** and they will need to apportion it out as best they can.

"In response to public demands", authorities have announced that plans have been prepared for the provision of **six** housekeepers to be available in Sydney to help families.

Householders will be placed **on their honour today** to reduce consumption of gas and electricity **by 20 per cent**. Public co-operation in **the voluntary plan** is required, it is stated, or compulsory measures will be introduced. As it turned out, there was virtually no reduction in usage.

A dental mechanic in Sydney's Parramatta was fined 103 Pounds for having **stolen 13 head of cattle from a farmer nearby**.

A hotel licensee was sentenced to **one month's imprisonment with hard labour** by the Federal Tribunal for having sold a bottle of Australian whisky for 50 Shillings, 36 Shillings above the fixed price....

Fines were often set for breaches of licencing regulation. **Prison was occasionally set, but common enough. Drinkers who were caught on licenced premises were regularly fines or jailed.**

JUVENILE DELINQUENTS

Worries about children continued to plague Letter-writers. Now attention switched to somewhat **less draconian punitive measures, and more towards the control of young people on the verge of delinquency**. Much of what they wrote about concerned the vices displayed during attendance at movies.

Letters, A Mother of Two. As one step towards better guidance, I suggest that suburban cinemas' Saturday afternoon programmes should consist of items suitable for children, as they form the major part of this audience, and that children under 16 should not be allowed to attend the evening performance unless accompanied by an adult. I know of too many youngsters of nine years who go several times each week to an 8pm to 11pm performance, as well as to the matinees, and their conception of a "smart guy" is one who can knock down or short up someone else without himself getting hurt, taking what he wants without paying for it, growling in their throats, and swaggering.

Also, while hordes of children in other countries are dying from starvation, it is a very common thing here to see children at cinemas, mouths bulging with lollies, an ice cream cone in one hand, and a couple of toffee apples in the other. Money is easily come by these days, but is that a reason for teaching the children to become squanderbugs?

Letters, Mother. "Just a Teacher" hits the nail on the head. Because corporal punishment was used unreasonably in older times many people consider there is no need for it at all now. The lax discipline of today is doing far more harm to our young people than has ever resulted from too strict a discipline, and this applies just as much to girls as to boys, if not more so.

Take the trouble to talk to girls found guilty of loose moral practices, so prevalent these days, and you will find that the factor contributing most to their lapse is the failure of their parents to do more than talk when the daughters misbehave. Most of these girls will admit they would not have gone wrong if they had had as a deterrent the knowledge that when they misbehaved they would be given a dose of strap.

Study the effects of the different methods adopted by parents in dealing with their daughters, and you will find that most teenage girls need a discipline they can feel, to keep their behaviour in reasonable bounds. Go into the homes where corporal punishment is used judiciously and not haphazardly, and you will find the girls are happy and contented, well-behaved, and easy to live with. Go into the home where corporal punishment is taboo, and you will find in many cases the girls are bad-tempered and unco-operative, and rudeness to parents and squabbles amongst themselves are every-day affairs.

Used wisely and with discrimination, corporal punishment has more in its favour than any other method of discipline.

Letters, Ralph Gottliebsen. Letters have not outlined the cause of the rapid growth of this problem and a constructive plan to meet it. The plain facts are: (a) Thousands of married women have entered industry, leaving many more thousands of children without proper care. (Leichhardt 750 children; Balmain 500 children, are examples.) (b) Existing child care facilities are hopelessly inadequate and cannot cope with one-tenth of the need.

Is it any wonder that 1942 was a record year for delinquency figures, and that 1943 will exceed that record? To those who say, "Put the women back in the home," it must be obvious that this is impossible without entirely disrupting our war effort. The fact is we will want more and more women in industry before victory is won. We had serious delinquency troubles before the war, and even now a large percentage of wayward children are coming from homes where family life is intact.

There is only one cure for this state of affairs. The Federal Government must set up a central Child Care Bureau to administer and subsidise **a network of child centres** wherever needed throughout the Commonwealth; these to be operated through State Education Departments and local councils. An emergency scheme would requisition existing suitable buildings and sites, or erect prefabricated structures in preparation for a much more comprehensive scheme in post-war reconstruction. Emergency personnel training courses should also be inaugurated immediately.

The cultural influences of **day nurseries, nursery schools, and play centres** will more than counter-balance the effects of temporarily broken homes and crime pictures. They will not only protect the child's health, education, and morale, but give guidance and instruction to those who most sorely need it.

Letters, Parent. Every parent is master of his own child until it reaches a certain age, and holds the key to what pattern that child is going to take. Reproof, plus corporal punishment, should be administered by the parent when necessary, and should not be left to school teachers and others. Many people use punitive measures with success, but the trouble is they leave off just when it is most necessary. Wayward youths and girls of today are the fruits of apathy, being vastly different from those of the Victorian era, who were checked until they became prudence itself.

Letters, Grandmother. It is indeed gratifying that at last steps are being taken to control Saturday afternoon matinees for children. Horror pictures should definitely be taboo. Another reform, long overdue, is better control of children in the theatres to check the head-splitting noises of the unruly children. The youngsters, these days, seem to be a law to themselves. They should be made to respond to discipline, and not allowed to litter the seats and floor with sweets and papers. The film-managers could cooperate and issue orders from the screen, by stopping the picture for a space, if necessary, to maintain order.

Comment. As you will see, **many** of the writers made sense, but it is noticeable that quite a number seemed to be ignoring the reality that most children loved things like spooky movies, and they liked making lots of noise on Saturday afternoons at the flickers. Equally, they would hate being dragged along to see stuff that was educational and good for them. Boys will be boys, and girls will be girls.

HATING AN EMPIRE

A clergyman at a conference in the NSW city of Wollongong stated as his theme that he "hated an Empire." As it was reported in the Press, it came out as though he hated **the British Empire**, and would willingly do away with it. He later explained that this remarks were **not directed at the current British Empire**, and that he meant that dominant nations should, in the post-war future, move away from their Empires and establish independent nations in their stead. There were many people who also thought this way so that his remarks were not as controversial as it was initially thought.

Still it raises the question of what Australians thought about imperialism, and for them, that meant what did they think about the British Empire? There is no doubt that **this** nation was **almost fanatical for its support for Britain in the war, and by inference, in support for its Empire.** The whole idea of the desirability of people with the same cultural background, speaking a single language, and having the same values, was unchallenged. Look at how it had worked in this war and in WWI. **The member nations had flocked to the Mother-country and saved it from disaster.** In return, all these same countries now did much or most of their trade with that Mother. To the benefit of all.

Look at how the Oz people were sacrificing themselves for the Brits right now. Oz Servicemen had given their lives to defend Britain right from the very beginning of the War. No one made them do this; they were all volunteers. Look at the rationing of sugar, butter, and (soon) meat. The only reason for rationing of these commodities in Oz was to provide for Britain. Look at the "Bundles for Britain" that Oz citizens sent off by the ship-load to Britain. These often contained goods that were very hard to get in Oz, such as tinned fruit, syrup, and condensed milk. No one made them do that. Then there was the support for the Empire Day holiday, and its wonderful Cracker night. Only the most jaded persons at this time were thinking that Oz should leave the Empire or, heaven forbid, that we should, in some ways, loosen out ties with the monarchy.

So, at the beginning of all public functions, and at movies, and at dances, at concerts in the village hall, and at school assemblies, *God Save the King* was played, and everyone stood up and kept quiet. It was obvious that there were quite a few thinkers who thought that, after the War, much of the Empire should be given independence and be allowed to form their own governments. India was the most obvious such nation, because it had the capacity to support itself and it almost had the means of governance already. But other nations of Africa, and the Pacific, should also be urged along the path to self-sufficiency.

This was not, however, needed for Australia, so most people thought. We already had our independence, our freedoms, our institutions of democracy, our egalitarianism, and our high standard of living. Let's stick with the Empire, trade with the Empire, take our migrants and war-brides from Britain, and get our innovations from Britain. To quit this, even for the flashy attractions now seen in America, was not on the Oz agenda.

Comment. As a young lad in 1943, I loved the British Empire. In my classroom, at a small school in the Cessnock coalfields, we had a single map, and that was on the wall near the front of the class. On a windy day outside, the map would flap and flap until it had to be taken down. It was a map of the world, and the possessions of the Empire were shown in the famous pink ink.

I was very proud to be part of that Empire. I could tell you who the British Empire boxing Champions were, and the Wrestling ones as well. I knew the fabulous titles of the rulers of various exotic nations, and what products they grew and exported to each other. I longed for the day when the War would be over, and the Brits, with their wonderful navy, could take over more lands, and the pink on the map would spread wider and wider.

Little did I know that the Empire by then had passed its peak. At the end of the war, all roads were downward. It had no money, was in deep debt, and many nations within it were desperately keen to throw off its yoke. If the citizens of the Roman Empire still occupied Britain, they would doubtless wisely attest that "Sic transit gloria" which, of course, I won't offend you by translating.

ABORIGINES

Letters, A Tryer. We are constantly reading of the shortage of domestic labour in hospitals while there are hundreds of aboriginal girls who would be pleased to take up this work, or other work that would help the war effort. We have one aboriginal girl taking a maternity course in Sydney. She was given her opportunity by the Church of England authorities, and proved a worthy pupil. I think it is time that these people were given the opportunity to see what they can do.

Letters, Ethel Richardson. I agree with "A Tryer" regarding aboriginal girls helping in hospitals. I have a semi-invalid in the home, and at different times I have had three aboriginal girls, one for seven years, and I always found them clean, honest, and, above all, they had **a white heart**.

Letters, Harry P Reynolds, The Rectory, West Goulburn. Recently I visited the Cootamundra Training Home for aboriginal girls, which is controlled by the Aborigines' Protection Board. There in pleasant surroundings, are 50 happy-looking girls and young women, cared for by a devoted and competent staff. I was told that the people of Cootamundra take a kindly and generous interest in the home and that a short time ago a State Minister promised additional necessary facilities. All of which, in view of our past dealings with the aborigines, was very encouraging.

There was, however, a vital question to which no satisfactory answer could be found. What is the policy of the board as representing Australia for the future of those girls? Most of them are well developed physically and the majority of them would be half-castes. When the time comes for them to leave the home, employment is found for them, usually as domestics. Through no fault of their own, but because of the views of the world in which they must live, their lot then must often become complex and menacing. I understand that a similar home for boys and youths who, as they reach manhood, will also need the companionship and the possible closer relationship of the opposite sex of their own race, is **some hundreds of miles away.**

I am aware that the solution to the problem may not be found easily but I am also convinced that the present arrangement, despite its many desirable features, cannot be expected to work satisfactorily. We have tardily awakened to our grave responsibility for our aborigines. Is there not a great deal more that we could be doing in an understanding way?

Letters, M Shannon, Nebo, Qld. I am a cattle pastoralist in north-west Queensland, where aborigines are still relatively plentiful, and an employer of them. My opinions are the result of a lifelong first-hand experience.

There is a future for these people if educated for economic independence. The aboriginal is a born herdsman and horseman and bushman. He has a natural skill with all manual tools. I have in my employment a pure-blood aboriginal who is an excellent carpenter, blacksmith, and a good farrier and saddler – all self-taught or "picked up" from white men. He also taught himself to read and write with fair facility. He may be above average in intelligence, but not exceptional. I have known many quite as good as he. The women are quite up to the men. They are particularly good with dairy cattle. They have the knack of friendliness with animals.

My contention is that aboriginal education should be designed to **fit the individual to be a skilled craftsman or an independent farmer or grazier. At present he has no chance.** In my own state he may not hold land in his own right. The local policeman is a very important man "outback," and the aborigines are proud that he is their friend. **But he controls their savings.** The employer is bound to pay about **four-fifths of the wages earned direct to the police,** to be paid into the employee's savings bank account. The police readily allow withdrawals for the employee's necessaries, or what they consider necessaries. I give my sincere commendation to the Queensland police for the manner in which they carry out this humane duty, but it does seem to me to cut the ground from under any effort to permanently solve the future of the aborigines.

The man in my employment to whom I have already referred has, I am told, about 750 Pounds to his credit. He asks: "What good is it to me? I cannot even buy a second-hand motor car or a buckboard and horses to go walkabout when I want to. Any white man who works no harder than I, can do as he pleases."

One feature in my district gives hope – the aboriginal full-bloods are increasing, and also half-castes are very rare. I do not know of any.

Comment. These letters show that some of advanced thinkers were becoming vocal on Aboriginal matters. All of the above writers are sympathetic to the aborigines, and clearly knew they were a long way from becoming equal to the whites, and also wanted to change that situation. These well-wishers, however, were not typical of the general population.

To the ordinary person, aborigines were seen as definitely second-class citizens. They were seen as being generally dependent on various Boards and hand-outs, as being dirty and destructive of property, as being bad drunks who would drink metho, as being violent, as fouling public swimming pools.

There were all sorts of stories, given wide circulation, of how various attempts to help aborigines backfired. For example, a common one was the way they destroyed white-man's houses if they were allowed to dwell in them. Another story was that **half-castes** were particularly bad, especially males.

The Letter-writers above were clearly not persuaded by these accounts. They had different ideas and were keen to do something, but you can see that their suggestions were very sketchy, and they were by no means offering **policy** decisions that effect **major** change. In this respect, **they were typical of reformers at the time.**

Still, they were at the vanguard of others who would slowly, ever so slowly, change their attitude to aborigines, to the stage where they are **now regarded (in 2020, say)** not as inferior, but rather as **citizens** who need more support than the **carrot-and-stick short-terms expedients given grudgingly by various vote-hungry governments.**

OTHER MATTERS

Letters, Florence Harris. It is now over 19 months since the fall of Singapore, and, with the exception of a small number of names **announced over the Japanese-controlled radios, nothing whatever has been learned of the fate of those of our Army nurses, about 60 in number – my own daughter is amongst them – who were not returned from that theatre of war.**

No prisoner of war cards have, so far as I am aware, been received from any of them, either in this or other States. The only official information I have been able to glean comes from (a) an aide of General Gordon Bennett, who stated on his return to Australia (18 months ago) that he – General Bennett – had arranged for the return transport of these nurses, and that they should now be on their way home; (b) from the Department of the Army "that they had no knowledge of their whereabouts or circumstances," and later, "that everything possible was being done to obtain such information."

It might be some source of comfort to the parents of these girls if they were informed of just what has been done by the Army authorities. Has any effort been made, or is it practicable, to make inquiries over the national short-wave radio? Have particular inquiries been made on this subject through the "protecting power"?

Letters, Christine Evans. Surely the time has arrived when action rather than talk is necessary. Everyone agrees that someone or something is to blame for the fearful depraved conditions which exist in society. It is high time we told our various Governments that war-time prohibition is the solution of the existing depravity. Surely we owe it to those young people, who should be in training for post-war reconstruction, to bring it about.

There can be no real rebuilding in the peace days if the drink traffic is to hold the same place in our country's life as it does now. It is somewhat unreasonable to blame the State for neglect of the young. It is really a reflection on our homes, schools, and churches rather than on the State. Christians have not been determined enough in their efforts to eradicate destructive forces which exist.

Australia stands at the cross-roads today: if we as a nation do not improve morally and spiritually there is nothing in the future but to become a decadent nation –we are heading that way.

Letters, David Hunter, Legislative Assembly, Sydney. Since war broke out great strides have been made in the production of plastics and their everyday use. It must be expected that **they will play a dominant part in post-war economy.** That may be generally good, but we in Australia have some reason to fear their in-roads.

It is to be hoped, therefore, that those responsible for post-war planning will pay particular attention to the following: **One.** What plastics will be produced outside Australia that will affect our economy? **Two.** What plastics can be produced within the Commonwealth for home and export markets? **Three.** What new primary products can be grown in Australia that will be used in their manufacture? **Four.** The effects synthetic foods may have on national health. **Five.** The effects of plastics generally on employment.

NOVEMBER NEWS ITEMS

A *SMH* staff correspondent says that **unseemly conduct** by Servicemen and young girls, under the influence of liquor in the city in the early hours of the morning, **is causing much concern** to police and volunteer welfare workers.

The revised Commonwealth **munitions programme** means that **less copper** will need to be mined. **Stocks** of this metal are described as **high**. **The effort needed for the War is decreasing** in many industries.

The Treasury will not approve investments in real estate in future unless the purchaser had made what are considered satisfactory investments in war loans.

The Treasury has provided a scale to be used for purchasers. If the sale price is **below 500 Pounds, there is no requirement** to subscribe. At 500 Pounds sales price, the requirement is 100 Pound subscription. And so on. **At 7,000 Pounds, the requirement is 5,000 Pounds.**

The purchaser **may not sell his bonds to pay for the land**. He **may not sell his bonds after the sale**, without Treasury permission – which will never be given. (The basic wage is about five Pounds).

33 were missing, and 1,414 were wounded. The War was much further away from our shores, but **it was still taking a dreadful toll**.

A Saturday parade of **munition workers and their products** through the main streets of Sydney showed that the production in factories **had moved from guns and munitions** on **to ships, locomotives and engines**.

The names of **511 Australian POW's**, released from **Axis captivity in Europe,** were published today. An exchange was made in neutral Spain, and an **equal number of German and Italian troops** were returned to their homelands. The men have arrived in Egypt, and **will come to Oz** as soon as shipping is made available.

A staff of special officers will be used in **a campaign** organised by the Feds **for the detection and punishment of black market offenders.**

At the opening of the Australian **Newspaper Proprietors' Association conference**, the president said that the problems of **censorship, and the difficulty of presenting a truthful picture** of the war, **still confronted** Oz newspapers.

During the **last three months**, **80 German U-boats** have been sunk. That brings the total for the last six months to 150. The **Allies are winning the battle of the Atlantic at last.**

The Minister for the Army announced that **19,927 Australian** soldiers originally listed as **missing** have been traced. The number **now listed as missing is 3,421. Big numbers.**

Children leaving school at the end of the year **will be allowed to take their annual holiday before registering** at National Services offices.

10 HIT SONGS FROM AMERICA

As Time Goes By	Rudy Vallee
Comin' in on a Wing and Prayer	Song Spinsters
Don't Get Around Much Anymore	Ink Spots
I Had the Craziest Dream	Harry James
Moonlight Becomes You	Bing Crosby
People Will Say We're in Love	Frank Sinatra
Stormy Weather	Lena Horn
That Old Black Magic	Glenn Miller
When the Lights Go on Again	Vera Lynn
You'd Be Nice to Come Home To	Dinah Shore

10 MOVIES RELEASED

Casablanca	Bogart, Bergman
Watch on the Rhine	Paul Lucas, Bette Davis
The Song of Bernadette	Jennifer Jones
For Whom the Bell tolls	Cooper, Bergman
Bataan	Robert Taylor
Destination Tokyo	Cary Grant
A Guy Named Joe	Tracey, Irene Dunne
Coney Island	Betty Grable
Girl Crazy	Rooney, Garland

WOMEN IN THE WORK-FORCE

The Director-General of Man-Power said that there were 845,000 women now in the work force. Of these, 644,000 were already in the workforce at the outbreak of War.

Thus, 200,000 had entered since the outbreak, and of these 90,000 say they would have entered if there had been no war. That means that 110,000 had been motivated by the war. Plus the 50,000 women in Auxiliary Services.

Comment. You might say that Man-Power had been moderately successful in recruiting women for duties. I am a bit more cynical and suggest that of the 160,000 actually recruited, about 160,000 would have helped out of their own volition.

MONDAY IS WASHING DAY

In 1943, almost all women, right across Australia, woke with a song in their hearts, because today was washing day. My Mum was no exception. Here at last was the day when all of the family's washing got a good soak and was then sorted into categories, and made ready for the copper. This wonderful piece of technology was a large copper hemi-spherical bowl, three feet across, set in concrete, with enough room underneath for a fire. Dad's role in the whole ritual was to chop enough wood the night before to allow Mum to keep the home fire burning for all Monday. Also, because there were no taps over the copper, he filled the copper with buckets of water.

Mum started by boiling coloured. Because of War-time shortages, there was no washing powder (detergents were unheard of), so good old Mum had to shave off scraps from a bar of Sunlight soap. After prodding and turning the coloureds for a quarter an hour, with the copper-stick, they were then extracted with the stick, and lumped into the cold-water tub. The clothes at this stage were coming from boiling water, spraying steam and hot water everywhere, so this transfer to the cold-tub was approached with caution. "Get back, Ronny. No …. Further…. No, further still."

In the cold-tub, clothes were bashed to get the dirty water from the copper out of them, and then moved to an adjacent tub, for rinsing with fresh cold water. Then they were taken out, piece by piece, and hand-strangled wickedly in the quaint process of wringing-out. They then made their way, rejoicing at their own cleanliness, to a cane washing-basket, and were ready for hanging out on a clothes line in the back-yard, complete with a clothes prop and wooden pegs.

Mum then went back, stoked the fire, emptied the dirty water out of the copper, and re-filled it and went on to "the whites". And so on. Mums all over Oz went through this ritual every week, and if you had a largish family, it really was exhausting. Then it was followed up on Tuesday with ironing day, and Thursday with cleaning day. Sunday was mainly cooking day, and this saw the production of sponge cakes, occasional fruit cakes, jelly-lamingtons, cream-puffs, and English caramels.

After that, of course, it was Monday again. "Keeping house" in those days was a pretty tough routine, with no washing machines, dryers, wringers, Hills Hoists, cars for the shopping and the kids, vacuum cleaners, non-press clothes, and a whole host of other benefits now available. But, **then,** even if you had the money to buy some of them, they were no longer available because of the War, and in fact, once they got sick there were no spare parts or mechanics, so they died. There was no way to escape.

I must add that today, in 2020, when I hear the occasional woman talking about how hard her job as a Mum is, I put on what my family describes as "my bland look." Of course, I rejoice in the fact that modernity in domesticity has long been here, and all the labour-saving devices are available. Not I, nor anyone, would wish to return to the Wash Days of 1943. It just seems however, that whether I like it or not, my memories flash to my Mum's days over the tubs, and I wish that things had been a lot easier for her and others.

RAMBLINGS

Having said that, I should add that sometimes I also think of my Dad. He was a miner, not just on Mondays, and shoveled 16 to 24 tons of coal a day, depending on his darg. In fact, six days a week, at this time. I won't dwell on it, but times down the pits were tough too, and dangerous. The point to all this is that when we oldies say some things were better in the past, we should also remember that there were many things that most certainly were not.

Let me close this Section by pointing out that things were a bit tough for this 9-year-old boy in 1943. I explain that all the kids nearby, about a dozen of us, before going to the pictures on a Saturday arvo, would walk bare-footed on a gravel road up to Kohler's shop, three-quarters of a mile away. We each had threepence, and stood with our noses to the front glass of the shop, and pointed to the lollies we wanted, ready for the pictures. These were **real** lollies. Musk sticks, bulls-eyes, licorice cigarettes, Nestles' penny chocolates, sherbet cones, jelly beans and licorice all-sorts. Sometimes a penny toffee, or a toffee apple.

This was up until 1942. After that however, lollies started to disappear from the window. It was sometimes said that a sugar shortage was to blame, but we all knew that the love of austerity for austerity's sake was behind it all. In any case, by the end of 1943, we all went off to the flickers **without** our lollies. Thankfully, the movies we loved were still to be seen.

What about Tarzan and Sabu, and Abbott and Costello in the Mummies' Tomb, and Rio Rita? Hope and Crosby on the Road to all sorts of exotic places, and Red Skelton as the Fuller Brush Man? Tom and Jerry cartoons? And the cowboy serials that ended each week with a damsel in distress. These were generally shown as the **first** session, before the interval. After the interval, the quality fell off a bit, though strangely some adults only came for the **second** half. Then, as America got more involved in the War, there was an increasing coverage of this. It was always comforting to see American victories – one after the other. But, even with all the sentimental muck that the oldies liked, it was great fun. I can recommend it to you. Get your little bag of lollies, and try it one Saturday afternoon.

FOUR INTERESTING LETTERS

Letters, I Sutton. This should be an opportune time to legislate for registration of builders so that when the post-war housing starts the public will be protected from jerry-builders. A plumber or an electrician must have a licence, so why not a builder? The Sydney Technical College have a building and construction course for which they give a higher trade certificate, but it is difficult to persuade a boy to serve an apprenticeship and give up all week nights to attend the Sydney Technical College for five years to receive a certificate that is not recognised.

Letters, Mrs Alice Grey. While the National Service is calling for ice makers and carters, the Department of War Organisation will not, I understand, permit the manufacture of the ordinary domestic ice chests. Surely, in the interest of economy, food preservation, and the encouragement of cold dishes (to save fuel), ice chests should be made available. What means is there of preserving ice without a chest?

Letters, H E McIntosh, Racial Hygiene Association of NSW, Sydney. Health Week is on, but so far no suggestion has been made for compulsory education of children of all ages in physiology, biology, or anatomy. Each child is in possession of an engine, the most complicated in the world, without the slightest instructions as to its care. We should be considered lunatics if we had put a man in charge of the Melbourne Express, who had not had education in the working of locomotives. Why not wake up and give similar instructions to our youth?

Letters, A Walsh. It was with astonishment and indignation that I read in your columns that seven South Australian members of a field ambulance have been sent to rejoin their unit in New Guinea, after only 14 days' leave, **after being prisoners of war for two years**. Evidently I am very simple, in that I did not realise that only returned politicians are feted, and only miners and slaughtermen are presented with holidays.

MEAT RATIONING

By this stage of the war, most people had been so badgered by authorities that they accepted new impositions without too much clamour. It all depended on whether or not the new rule was reasonable. Right now, then, most Letter-writers clearly thought that sending our meat to help Britain was reasonable enough, and thus their reaction to the **impending meat rationing** was muted. Still, quite a few Letters turned up, and I leave you to digest their wisdom.

Letters, Suggesting. Meat rationing is looming over us – but, recognising the need of those who have suffered so much more than we have, few will grumble at the rationing, or at the amount given us. May I plead, however, for a simpler method of rationing, in the interests of both the busy butcher and the worried housewife? If the 2¼lb are to be covered by a single coupon, then (in spite of statements to the contrary), the housewife will be virtually limited to the one butcher. The butcher will have the extra trouble of recording the credit outstanding when **a coupon is broken** and the buyer must return to that butcher to complete the coupon.

This will prevent the occasional buying to advantage of which the careful housewife likes to avail herself. With deliveries cut out, the hard-pressed housewife has to make do with the little local butcher, almost all the time. But perhaps once a month she gets a day in town, or a visit to a larger shopping centre. Here, just once in a while, she has a chance to gaze into an attractive butcher's window display and is reminded of that occasional titbit, or that cheap joint which never seems available at the little humdrum shop. But she will not be able to avail herself of this opportunity **without laying out her whole coupon**, and it may be long ere she can come again to claim the credit allotted to her.

There are plenty of pages of coupons in our books. Instead of having one coupon cover the whole week's ration, why not allow one coupon to each ½lb of meat (or small number of points, if these are used). Then the housewife will be able (literally) to buy wherever it is most convenient at the time, surrendering coupons according to the weight to the nearest half-pound – and the busy butcher will be saved extra book recordings. The method of rationing is not yet finalised, so perhaps this suggestion may be in time to receive consideration and thus help to prevent one more limitation being placed on the already so harassed housewife.

Letters, Kerema. Now that meat rationing is decided upon, will the Rationing Commission enlighten us as to what is to take the place of meat? Bacon is unprocurable. Fish, owing to the price, is out of the question. Fruit is, too, for the same reason. Finally, the price of vegetables is absurd.

Letters, H Chidgey It is stated that there will be no meat available for animals. It is rather dreadful to think that these creatures, who are dependent upon us for the right to live and to eat, are to be denied food. After all, human beings can vary their diet. I think it is very much to the discredit of human beings that, even in times of stress, some thought cannot be given to the animals, who have been something to us, either by their devotion or, in many instances, their use.

Lack of meat for the cats and dogs will simply mean that, in the majority of cases, the animals will be thrown onto the streets or sent off to be lethalised, in which case the rats will come into their own, and with them the disease that they so generously distribute. And there can be no rationing or distribution of disease: this chooses its own victims and distributes itself.

Letters, Harry Edwards. I point out to Dorothy Parks that people are not complaining much about meat rationing. They know that it is going to our Motherland, where it is very much needed.

I know personally that Malta had it hard. And that we are well off compared to there at that time. But even if we complained a lot – and I claim we do not – there would be a purpose to doing that. **Firstly**, it makes us feel better. **Secondly,** if we whinge a lot, maybe our rulers will heed us, and relax their over-zealous rules sooner rather that later. **Thirdly**, it alerts smart operators to the problem, and that encourages them to offer alternative solutions. Some times, via the black market.

There is nothing virtuous or courageous about suffering in silence. I know first-hand that the people of Malta did not.

OTHER MATTERS

Letters, J Earnshaw, Roseville. The time is ripe for legislation to prevent **further cruelty to humans by domestic animals**. The continual barking dog is perhaps the most common, the most aggravating, and the least controlled of the noises that disturb the quiet and repose of homelife. An appeal to the owner in most cases falls on deaf ears and authority is indifferent. Yet if any person carried on a trade or occupation in a residential area and caused a far less annoyance to his neighbours, the law would be swift to deal with the offender. Fierce and loud-barking dogs are an anachronism in the modern city and should be relegated the lonely farmhouse and the pasture.

CHRISTMAS IS COMING

All the agencies involved in providing comforts for our servicemen overseas made special efforts at Christmas. Hampers with lots of goodies were one way of doing this, even though they were often delivered months late.

Letters from home were the most prized, and these too were uncertain in their timing.

A typical Christmas hamper contained a tin of Cream of Chicken soup, roast turkey, roast pork, baked potatoes, both with apple sauce. Vegies were supplied in the form of cauliflower and parsnips, with brown sauce. Desserts took the form of Xmas Pudding, with brandy sauce, and also mince pies and jam tarts.

For afters, there was cheese fingers and coffee.

Then to the hard stuff. Cigarettes, beer and wine, followed by nuts and dates. All suitably packaged in Chrismas wrappings.

In large bases overseas, it was sometimes possible to put on a slap-bang feast. Next day, it was probably back to watery cabbage and scrambled eggs made from powder.

CULTURAL INFLUENCE OF THE YANKS

The US forces brought with them some of their most prized adjuncts to a full life. Among these were coca cola, chewing gum, and bubble gum, goof caps, zoot suits, and of course, **pin-ups**.

These works of art were displayed in all the places that the Yanks went. In their barracks, on the cock-pits of their planes, and on their jeeps. The ladies photographed were often film stars. A particular favourite was **Betty Grable**.

DECEMBER NEW ITEMS

The Man-Power directorate is to begin the **compulsory** recruitment of single girls to work as domestics **in hospitals.**

Mr Curtin said that Oz had undertaken to **give Britain 35 per cent of its butter production, and 22 per cent of its egg production**. He stated that the public was the only authority that could stamp out black marketing. He urged the **cheerful acceptance of food rationing.**

Mr Curtin also said a few days later that Australians should avoid "**an orgy of unrestrained and foolish Christmas spending**". War Savings Certificates would make the best gift, he said.

Fights occurred in several hotels last Saturday when **publicans refused to serve schooners of beer** to their customers. Middies (in a smaller glass) are more profitable.

A pedestrian walking at the top of Dover cliffs reported seeing **bluebirds over the white cliffs.**

Thirteen Wolf Cubs were drowned when they **fell from a punt** in which 28 Cubs and three Boy Scouts were crossing the Clarence River at Grafton on Saturday. Frightened by choppy waters, the boys had crowded to one side of the punt, which tilted and flung them into the river. Floodlights were turned on as the light faded, and thousands watched until the last body was recovered, at 10 pm.

Japanese leaders are convinced that **only a desperate spurt in the war effort** made at any cost will save them.

This is the message from the *SMH* Correspondent at Chunking. He said that expansion of Japan's war industry was made possible only by **exploiting the people, who are overworked and underfed**. This is remarkably **similar to the position in Australia**, especially a few months ago.

In preparation for a major winter offensive, the Russians are training 380,000 **ski troops**.

Hundreds of cases of spirits, obtained by the pretence that they were for troops in New Guinea, had been sold on the black market. The perpetrators were appearing before a Federal Special Court.

The Feds announced that munitions workers will be given a continuous **10 days Christmas holiday**. That's a lot better than **nil** days last Christmas.

The NSW Chief Secretary has given permission for an Arts Union lottery that will raise money for the **Sheepskins for Russia appeal.**

Heavy mortality among caged birds is reported by leading breeders. They believe that **diseased thistle seed** is the cause.

The US Army announced that there was no way in which an enlisted **member of the US Army** could **avoid paying maintenance** to his Australian wife and family.

Seven people were injured by a **steel cable trailing from an aircraft** which was flying low over a beach near Sale in Victoria. **One girl had both legs severed.**

NEWS FROM THE WAR FRONTS

The end of 1943 saw the Allied forces in very good positions. The Russians to the east of Europe had fought back from the point of calamity to the stage where they were nearing their own borders. For example, in Poland, they were getting close to the heartland, and in the Ukraine they had recaptured some of the territory that they had ceded a year ago.

The war in Africa was just a distant memory, and British and American Armies were well up towards the Alps, and slowly pushing forward, despite the seasonal floods and mud. In Greece and Yugoslavia, **Resistance groups** were tying up large numbers of Germans, and were getting more troublesome by the day.

In the air, the Allies were bombing western Europe almost non-stop. Berlin was being hammered, French ports likewise, and submarine bases were copping heaps. Italian cities were on the target lists, and strategic spots in Norway and Denmark got their fair share. The **Battle of the Atlantic**, against the subs, was going better than it ever had, and looked like coming to an end in the next few months.

In all, it looked like **the Allies in Europe were set for a victory.** There was all sorts of talk about starting a Second Front somewhere on the western edges of Europe, though with winter setting in there was little scope for this at present. In any case, such a venture would need extremely careful planning, and that would take months from here. Perhaps an Allied invasion in mid-1944 might be on the cards.

In the south-west Pacific, Australian troops had spent all of 1943 finishing off the Japanese who had entrenched themselves all along the northern coast of New Guinea. These forces were well dug-in, and getting rid of them, almost man-by-man, took a savage toll on our troops. The Air Forces of Australia and the US spent the year bombing Japanese-occupied places in the Marshall, Gilbert and Solomon Islands, with an ever-increasing number of islands falling to our armies. All was pretty good in the Pacific, as well.

Comment. Before leaving discussion of the War, I would like to mention **two matters**. **The first** is that while we had cause to rejoice over our remarkably improved military situation, reports of deaths and mutilations still kept coming through. There were still thousands and thousands of families every day who dreaded the coming of the postman, or the telegram boy. For them, and friends and neighbours, there could never be any peace of mind till the boys came home again – for good.

The second matter is that these fears were not restricted to just ourselves. About **14 million Russians troops were killed** in the War. 1943 was their year for slow, grinding victories, but it was also the year of their greatest number of deaths. Sometimes it is easy to forget those men who fell, and their families, but it might be better if we remembered that all of them (from every country involved) suffered in the same way as we in Australia suffered. **To me, no one wins a War; everyone is a loser.**

THE MEN AND WOMEN IN THE STREET

Ordinary Australians at the end of 1943 were relieved, and were no longer at all fearful of invasion, but they were not yet ready to dance in the street. They knew soberly that there was still a long way to go, and that rationing and overtime and austerities would still be part and parcel of their lives for at least another year. Still, they inevitably started to wonder about life after the War.

Some persons were doing more than wonder. For example, there were many politicians, ever-conscious of the votes that would come home with the soldiers, who were advocating preference in jobs and housing for returned servicemen. This meant that if two identical men applied for a job, or to occupy a house, then preference would go to the ex-serviceman. This was all well and good, but there already existed, in most States, a legislated preference for Trade Union members. What would happen in the example above if the apparent loser was a member of a Trade Union, and the ex-serviceman was not? Who would then get preference? You can see that there were many battles yet to be fought before that issue would be settled.

Others were **also** thinking about life after War. The Feds had set up a Department for Post War Reconstruction, all of the State governments were making grand promises that they would provide umpteen new houses for the returned Diggers, and that jobs would grow on trees. It sounded like a paradise for them, and surely they would respond by casting their votes wisely.

At this time, **about one Letter in six to the *SMH* was dwelling on post-War matters.** They were however, getting ahead of themselves, and I happen to know that there were plenty of vexing matters ahead in 1944, before the realities of the re-organisation of society became pressing.

OTHER MATTERS

Letters, W Downe. Ethelred the Unready was both unwise (unready) in expecting that the enemies whom he invited to assist him in a crisis would depart when the crisis was over and unready (through surprised) to cope with them when they returned uninvited.

We, too, apparently, imagine that we can adopt the principles and weapons of totalitarianism to fight totalitarianism and "get away with it." There are already abundant signs that this political disease, which has killed so many millions of soldiers and civilians in the last 10 years, but to which we ourselves so lightheartedly resort to "cure" any inconvenient problem, is already becoming chronic. Dr Lloyd Ross and the Chamber of Manufactures assure us that **restrictions on individual liberty must continue, or even be increased, after the war in order that liberty may continue and prosperity return.**

Thus in the beginning have all dictatorships been justified by the argument that they are necessary to preserve and "protect" liberty. It is irrational and illogical to believe that liberty and prosperity can be preserved or restored by a dose of tyranny and restrictions.

Letters, A Huie. Dr Lloyd Ross has been talking. He has given us a preview of the Servile State which the Government proposes to set up after the war. He said: "We must have planners and bureaucrats." He wants controls and restrictions placed upon liberty. This is the very antithesis of a **sound after-war policy**. It reveals the **socialistic itch to meddle in the affairs of the people** instead of allowing them freedom to attend to their own business.

We have a multitude of boards and committees now with irksome and harassing restrictions. The government does not know what it costs to administer them, let alone the appalling losses caused to producers. The poor work of the Apple and Pear Board is a case in point. In Victoria its follies have been so disastrous that a State, which once had apples for export, is not supplying its own needs.

Manpower and petrol can be found to send men round harassing back-country farmers as to the number of hens they have. The great wrong of employing planners and bureaucrats is that of making crimes of action which are not sins – actions naturally moral and economic. The general public is aware of the appalling incompetence shown in a great many ways by these planners and bureaucrats which we are coolly told must continue to afflict us when the war ends.

Now we understand why the Federal Government wants increased powers. **It is anxious to keep the multitude of meddling officials, often with no knowledge of the business they are mis-managing, indefinitely.** I want to say as forcibly as I can that there is no need for increased Federal powers. I have pointed that out already to Dr Evatt. All that is necessary is understanding and courage to wisely use the powers that they have.

But that does not suit the present political and official mind. It wants a dictatorship over industry. It seeks to graft continental ideas of restrictions on a people nurtured in the principles of British liberty. No doubt Dr Ross will have no hesitation later in expanding the

present system of inspectors into a secret police.
We will then have the Servile State – planners and
bureaucrats ordering people about instead of allowing
them their natural rights and liberties. All this with
the pretence of employing the men after the war. I can
imagine no surer way to bring on a depression and
starve them.

HOUSING NEWS ITEMS

Letters, William R Laurie. Other letters on subdivisions
and similar subjects show that it is scarcely realised that
there is a trained occupation of town planner, which
has the technique to solve the problems worrying the
writers. If our existing buildings had had the benefit of
town planning legislation, and the consequent services
of trained town-planners, and had all our buildings
received full design analysis, many of our present
problems would never have arisen.

Whatever method is adopted in the handling of our
post-war building, one thing is certain. Unless each
particular type of fully-trained designer is allowed to
play his full part at every section of the work, from town
design to the details of kitchen equipment, the result
will be inefficient, unbeautiful, and extravagant.

News item. The full Federal Cabinet, after consideration
today of an interim report by the Commonwealth
Housing Commission, set a housing target of 50,000
houses in the first year after the war.

State Governments would be asked, the Prime Minister,
Mr Curtin, announced, to prepare plans for 30,000
Government-sponsored dwelling units for low-income
families as part of the 50,000 total (which includes
private building). The programme would be reviewed
annually.

Financial aid, Mr Curtin said, would be provided by the Commonwealth to the States to meet high building costs and provide rent rebates for persons with incomes below the basic wage or with large families.

AN INTERESTING VIEW OF CCC LIFE

Letters, D Stewart, Gen. Sec., WEA, Sydney. We have been advised by the Prime Minister that the Government does not consider that it should undertake the task of providing education facilities for workers in CCC camps.

That there is a need for such a service has been brought home to us by our own experience and by the correspondence we occasionally receive from old members now resident in CCC camps. Quoting from one such letter written by Mr Harry James, member of Rocky Creek Camp committee, CCC, he says: "Hundreds of workers are in camps throughout the State, sometimes miles from civilisation, with no transport, recreational, or educational facilities. Hence spare time is spent in playing cards, dice games, two-up or occasional bouts of metho-drinking to try and break the monotony."

In the early part of this year the Workers' Educational Association arranged a number of lectures for the CCC camp at St Marys. When negotiating for permission to enter the camp, we found a good deal of skepticism as to the possibility of any educational work being possible. This was well expressed by one personnel officer, who assured me that "all the men were interested in was their pay and a bellyful of beer." This certainly was not our experience at St Marys. We had an average attendance of 40 to 60 at our lectures, and the discussions at times were quite keen. We were forced to discontinue this work when the camp at St Marys was being broken up. It is impossible for this Association to even enter the camps in those outback areas. In our opinion the task is beyond the resources of any voluntary body. We would appeal to other organisations to support a request to the Commonwealth Government to reconsider its decision on this matter.

CHRISTMAS CHEER

Some months ago, some bright spark established regulations that said that shops and traders must not mention in their ads that the goods could be used for Christmas gifts. This was clearly to establish some level of misery that was thought to be good for the population. As it turned out, it appeared to have failed, and people went about their Christmas preparation with the same gusto as they always did. They were also cheered by the thought that this year most of them would get a few weeks of holidays as well as the Public Hols. One real problem was that many of the goods that were normally given as presents were **simply not available, even on the black market**.

Another was that many presents demanded the coughing up of **irreplaceable clothing coupons**, and there were scarcely enough of these to provide for a family's own needs, So poor old Dad had to do without his normal box of handkerchiefs, and even lucky cash-rich Mums missed out on the fox-fur stole that had been evident in earlier, more carefree, days.

In any case, there was still much activity, and I enclose just one Letter on the subject.

Letters, Grandmother. Anyone who has seen the misery and jealousy caused by one family having a number of costly toys and the adjoining family being too poor to provide some sort of toys for their children, will know that toys are necessary, to avoid spite, jealousy, and an inferiority complex, which perhaps will mar a child's future life. Psychologists declare that these small things exert a very wide and far-reaching effect on children's lives.

Another point is that the huge prices asked (and paid) must lower the amount of good food bought for the children in these homes. Experience over 40 years has shown me that the more expensive toys are frequently bought by people of thriftless habits, and that consequently bills are left unpaid or inferior food bought. Several small shopkeepers have told me personally that they consider the price asked at warehouses and large shops from which they buy their stock quite ridiculous, and out of all relation to the cost of the making of the articles.

SOME VISIONS OF THE FUTURE

Now I am at the stage of closing off a book, I generally indulge myself by **having a small rant.** So I hope you will bear with me for a few moments while I comment on a few matters that have slowly raised their head over 1943, and will become the subjects of much discussion in the future.

The direction of politics. Within Oz, over the course of the year, it was the role of Trade Union executives that had changed the most. When invasion was still a possibility at the beginning of the year, they were restrained, though very conscious of the power that they then had. Now, however, with the threat gone, some of them were fighting for the role they wanted to play in running the nation. Rank-and-file workers, like coal miners and wharfies, had little interest in the political objectives of their Union Executives, but they did appreciate the role they played in preserving working conditions. So when called upon to strike, they struck.

Some of these Executives were **inspired by Communism**, and wanted a nation that would be a micrcosm of Russia. Their idea was that, if over the years they could create enough industrial havoc, the current State would collapse, and the nation would turn to the severe tonic of State control of most aspects of life. The trouble for them was that those ordinary members who followed them into strikes, for better conditions, were not at all interested in destroying the State as it now was.

So, at the end of 1943, the scene was set for a great ideological battle that lasted for a decade or more. On the one hand, were the Communists, with Stalin as their god. On the other hand, was a new political Party, that was just emerging from the ruins of the United Party. The **new Party was the Liberal Party**, and within months it would be have **elected Bob Menzies as the Leader.** He would make anti-Communism the centre-piece of his philosophy, and milk that until he retired 20-odd years later.

Will we become a socialist State?   Many of the Labour politicians talking about life after the War were dead keen to set up a socialist State. This was not as extreme as a Communist State, but it did mean, say, that war-time constraints and planning and austerity would continue. It meant too that the Government might take control of some industries. After all, in Britain, the coal and steel-making industries were right now on the chopping block and, with a later change in Government, would succumb to Socialism. **Would not the economy be better off if we planned it**

more carefully, and if the Government could force people to go to places and do things they were not prone to do? Did we not escape from the clutches of the Japanese by all pulling together, and making sacrifices? Surely then, after the War, we should leave things as they are now, and let the State look after us.

As it turned out, the Labour Government after the war did make a fair effort to move to the splendour of the Socialist State. **It took an enormous length of time to remove the strictures and austerities imposed under the National Securities Act.** It maintained rationing for years, even for six years in the case of butter and petrol. It tried to nationalise the banks, even to the stage of a referendum. **The bureaucracies it had established had to be dragged screaming back to reality.** It was only after the success of the reds-under-the beds election campaign of Bob-Menzies in 1950 that the notion of socialism for this nation was replaced by an embryonic version of the American notion of capitalism and free-enterprise.

THE END OF 1943

At the end of 1943, people generally were much less worried about the War and were better off financially than a year earlier. They could see that some of the regulations might soon be relaxed, yet meat rationing was just **starting**, so they were in two minds over what austerities would be their lot. Their housing had deteriorated as a result of the effective ban on building, and the variety of goods in the shops had reduced. The news they got was still censored to ridiculous extremes. They could not buy Christmas presents like bicycles, cricket bats, French perfumes, decent soaps, indecent books, or replacements for anything.

They were thoroughly tired out from overwork, were fed up with the war, and just wished that it, and all talk of it, would go away. Still, this year, at least most of them could take a couple of weeks holiday. And there was always the hope that sometime, maybe even next year, the War would be all over, and everything would go back to normal. Without the shortages.

So that was the big message that came from the pulpit, the Letters columns, the politicians, and countless mums talking over the back fence. It was that peace was in sight, that our sons would come home and sleep in their own beds, that cars would be back on the roads with tyres on them, that lollies and chocolates and cakes with pink icing would be back in the shops, that air-raid shelters would be buried, that shirt tails would again be long enough, that **the lights would go on again, all over the world.**

COMMENTS FROM READERS

Tom Lynch, Speers Point…..Some history writers make the mistake of trying to boost their authority by including graphs and charts all over the place. You on the other hand get a much better effect by saying things like "he made a pile". Or "every one worked hours longer that they should have, and felt like death warmed up at the end of the shift." I have seen other writers waste two pages of statistics painting the same picture as you did in a few words….

Barry Marr, Adelaide….you know that I am being facetious when I say that I wish the war had gone on for years longer so that you would have written more books about it…

Edna College, Auburn…. A few times I stopped and sobbed as you brought memories of the postman delivering letters, and the dread that ordinary people felt as he neared. How you captured those feelings yet kept your coverage from becoming maudlin or bogged down is a wonder to me….

Betty Kelly. Every time you seem to be getting serious you throw in a phrase or memory that lightens up the mood. In particular, in the war when you were describing the terrible carnage of Russian troops, for no reason, you ended with a ten line description of how aggrieved you felt and ended it with "apart from that, things are pretty good here". For me, it turned the unbearable into the bearable, and I went from feeling morbid and angry back to a normal human being….

Alan Davey, Brisbane….I particularly liked the light-hearted way you described the scenes at the airports as the American high-flying entertainers flew in. I had always seen the crowd behaviour as disgraceful, but your light-hearted description of it made me realise it was in fact harmless and just good fun….

In 1940, the Brits had military disasters in Norway, Belgium and Tobruk. German subs were filling the Channel with British shipping. The Hun parked their planes full-time over London, and Blitzed it. But, against all odds, the Poms survived. In Oz, the first Menzies Government rationed food, clothing, petrol, smokes and shirt tails. It introduced conscription for men, and internment for Italian men. Photography was suspect, strikes were almost treason.

In 1941, in Europe, Hitler made his biggest mistake in the War when he invaded Russia. Churchill made his own big mistake when he sent Australian troops to the slaughter in Greece and Crete. In the Pacific, Japan was getting more frustrated as America cut off her resources by blockades. In Oz, we were shocked to the core when the Japs bombed Pearl Harbour in December. A Pacific War started, and Hitler made his second biggest blunder by siding with Japan. We in Australia could not believe that our own shores were under threat.

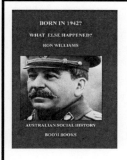

In 1942, Governments took over almost everything. Men were conscripted, and many sent to their death. Everything worthwhile was rationed, all private boats and yachts were seized by the navy. Jazz was giving way to crooners, like Crosby and Sinatra. Test cricket had gone, beer was very hard to get, and houses and cars were blacked out at night.

In 1944, the Japs in the Pacific and the Nazis in Europe was just about beaten. In Oz, the Labour Government delighted in having great war-time powers, and wanted to extend them. It took a referendum to cool them down. Sydney was invaded by rats, and there were lots of Yankee soldiers in all our cities, and a few of them were not hated. Young girls were being corrupted by the Yanks and by war-time freedom, and clergy were generous with their advice to them.

****

Chrissi and birthday books for Mum and Dad and Aunt and Uncle and cousins and family and friends and work and everyone else.

Don't forget a good read and chuckle for yourself.

In 1945, Germany was invaded, but that did not stop the Doodlebugs dropping on London. The Japs gave up and the Germans gave up. In Oz, every Jap was hated for the next twenty years at least. Bulldogging and buckjumping were quite popular, and the distinction between Communism and Socialism was not at all clear. The Brits were starving, and our own Bundles for Britain helped a lot. Rubber tyres for cars and bikes will be on sale next year, rationing of silk stockings will be abolished. Could the world get any better?

****

AVAILABLE FROM ALL GOOD BOOK STORES AND NEWSAGENTS